THREE HORSEMEN
OF
THE NEW APOCALYPSE

THREE HORSEMEN
OF
THE NEW APOCALYPSE

NIRAD C. CHAUDHURI

DELHI
OXFORD UNIVERSITY PRESS
CALCUTTA   CHENNAI   MUMBAI

Oxford University Press, Great Clarendon Street, Oxford OX2 6DP

Oxford New York
Athens Auckland Bangkok Calcutta
Cape Town Chennai Dar es Salaam Delhi
Florence Hong Kong Istanbul Karachi
Kuala Lumpur Madrid Melbourne Mexico City
Mumbai Nairobi Paris Singapore
Taipei Tokyo Toronto
and associates in
Berlin Ibadan

© *Oxford University Press 1997*

First published 1997
Third impression 1998

ISBN 0 19 564189 2

Typeset by S.J.I. Services, New Delhi 110 024
Printed in India at Pauls Press, New Delhi 110 020
and published by Manzar Khan, Oxford University Press
YMCA Library Building, Jai Singh Road, New Delhi 110 001

Preface

The very first thing I have to tell those who will read this book is that it is being written by a man in his ninety-ninth year (the date of his birth being 23 November 1897, the year of the Diamond Jubilee of Queen Victoria). I have never read or heard of any author, however great or productive in his heyday, doing that.

This confession alone will be enough to make the reader expect only senile babbling from me. It is not for me, however, to reassure him. He must be his own judge.

But I shall at least lay my cards on the table. In choosing the form of the book I have taken Machiavelli, Thomas Hobbes and Alexis de Tocqueville as my models. These great thinkers and writers were not given to looseness of thinking or imprecision in writing. Of these qualities I shall try to give an imitative display. But that is also likely to create mental resistance to what I shall say. Readers will anticipate both rigidity and aridity. I would, however, assure them that the dryness will be only in the form of the exposition, not in its substance. That is to say, the form of the book will have the same relation to its contents as the skeleton of an animal has to its full body. No vertebrate can stand without its bony structure but it is not the living animal without flesh and blood as well as the outermost integument.

Next, I shall inform the reader that I hold a very personal and to many an odd view of my authorship. It consists in thinking that I am not the real creator of my books but only the medium or amanuensis for the self-revelation of the subjects I deal with.

So far as it lies in my power, I have never allowed my likes or dislikes, my predilections and prepossessions to influence my presentation of my subjects. I have, so to speak, tried to keep the lens of my mind free from chromatic aberrations.

This has called for an exceptional effort on my part. That has been the case because throughout my long career as a writer, which began as far back as 1925, I have been an *engagé* fighting for causes. I would not admit that this has made me only a partisan writer. I have always held the view that the most effective partisan is he who never suppresses truth and who never shrinks from facing a reality. Yet whatever my own view of my vocation, readers in India have always attributed dogmatism, eccentricity and even arrogance to me. But how could I be half-hearted or apologetic about what I considered a gift and a revelation?

Finally, I would add that I have tried to make the book self-contained, so that the reader will not have to go to other books for finding the sources of the citations. This applies as much to the diction of my book as to its substance. Instead of saying that *le style est l'homme même,* I say *le style est le sujet même.*

This has necessarily made me a speaker of the *mot juste.* I often ponder for a long time over the words of a given passage, and I never sit down to write or type until I have the whole wording in my head. Therefore, the practical part of my writing has been very quick.

To an educated man, I hope, I shall not give any opening for misunderstanding me unintentionally. Nevertheless, if any genuine doubt arises I request the reader to get my meaning from the following dictionaries:

I. *The Oxford English Dictionary (OED)* to ascertain which historical sense I have adopted. The context will not leave any doubt as to that.

II. *The Webster International Dictionary* (2nd edition, 1936), with addition of new words to 1948, for current usage.

III. *The American Heritage Dictionary of the English Language,* 1969, for special American usage, although Webster also gives some of that.

After all these elaborate explanations, no one, I hope, will accuse me of sailing under false colours.

Oxford
30 March 1997   *Nirad C. Chaudhuri*

Contents

PART ONE

Of Method, Fundamental Assumptions, and State of Mind

Read not to contradict and confute, nor to believe and take for granted, nor to find talk and discourses, but to weigh and consider.

—Francis Bacon: *Essays,* 'Of Studies'

two post-mortem regions tells him that, being a pagan, he cannot take Dante any further. I give his words in Cary's translation:

> ... both fires, my son.
> The temporal and eternal, thou hast seen;
> And art arrived, where of itself my ken
> No farther reaches. I with skill and art
> Thus far have drawn thee. Now thy pleasure take
> For guide. O'ercome the steeper way
> O'ercome the straiter.
>
> > (*Purgatorio,* Canto XXVII, pp. 126–32)

But in actual fact Dante does not depend solely on his pleasure for the last journey. Just as he took Virgil as guide through Inferno and Purgatorio, he now takes Beatrice. Virgil was reason, Beatrice faith.

Virgil's words to Dante were these:

> ... expect no more
> Sanction of warning voice or sign from me,
> Free of thy own arbitrament to choose,
> Discreet, judicious. To distrust thy sense
> Were henceforth error.

My Fundamental Assumption about the Cosmos or Universe

I am speaking first about the universe because what happens in the mundane order, i.e. on earth and to mankind, is only an offshoot of the larger phenomenon and is contained in the larger framework. The two cannot be inconsistent with each other, even though the successive emergences might be wholly new. The antecedent and the successor remain indissolvably connected. To break that connection is not only to break the contact between the past and the present, but also to misunderstand the present. So, I have to set down my cosmic assumption first.

In regard to the universe, I have, on the one hand, accepted the theories of contemporary scientists and, on the other, rejected them.

The acceptance is about the nature of the universe, and the rejection about its duration.

Let me begin with the acceptance. It is now agreed among the scientists who devote themselves to cosmology that the universe is not a material body, nor has it a material structure. It is a process and a flow of energy in different directions. What that energy really is no one can say. It is perceived as light and heat by the sense organs of man and what creates both light and heat is conventionally called electricity. But, again, nobody can say what electricity is, its existence is deduced from the effects it produces.

The cosmos is perceived as a material body only by the sense organs of human beings; otherwise, it is the pattern in which energy works. In order to make this notion clear I shall quote what I wrote in an article published in the *Independent on Sunday* of 24 January 1990:

> Now the invention of television has finally given a practical demonstration of the truth of the scientific hypothesis, and put an end to the credibility of a material universe. On the one hand, there can be no doubt that what we see on the television screen is a pictorial representation of the things we see in our real life. On the other, there is equally no doubt that these images are produced by electricity in motion. On this analogy, it is permissible to hold that the universe is really a cosmic TV show run by some power who designed it for some purpose known only to itself.

Man's happiness lies in living on the strength of his illusions. It is the maya of the Hindu philosophy of Vedanta.

But I have wholly rejected the theory of modern scientists about the future existence of the universe. They have postulated a beginning for it; whether it was created by a 'Big Bang' or otherwise does not matter for my argument. The scientists, by merely assuming a beginning, were bound logically to postulate also an end. Actually, they have not been satisfied with a mere postulate. They have mathematically proved their hypothesis. It has been done with the help of the discipline of Thermodynamics, which has formulated as its Second Law that energy once lost in its application cannot be recovered. Therefore, the total energy of the universe will one day be lost and the universe will cease to exist.

My mind revolted against this mathematical law instinctively, and I regarded it as an expression of scientific Nihilism. Every human activity on earth and every achievement of man was rendered meaningless by it. It deprived all human achievement of its permanence, making it different for only a purposeless game. It rendered futile every creative and conservative effort of man, and made even the beneficial destructive function of civilized man totally unnecessary. Everything that man does becomes a tale told by an idiot signifying nothing.

Yet, with my firm trust in science I could not brush it aside. Torn between these two, I suffered because man cannot be happy without believing in the permanent existence of what he creates in pursuit of his ideals. Faith is necessary for man. That was why the Athanasian Creed began with the statement: *Quicunque Vult*—Whosoever will be saved: before all things it is necessary that he hold the Catholic faith. Which Faith except every one do keep whole and undefiled: without doubt he shall perish everlastingly. Even without the word 'Catholic' or 'Christian', the declaration would be true. Faith has no necessary connection with any established religion. Faith in human endeavour is enough.

My assumption about the duration of the universe might be right or it might be wrong. If it is wrong I lose nothing, simply stand where I stood. But should it be right I shall gain a good deal. In fact, even though my assumption remains unproved, I have gained. It has given me the will and energy to pursue my vocation of writer till I am almost a centenarian, although my tiny and frail body can supply only a small amount of it.

It has been for me like laying a wager, of which Pascal wrote. A number of his thoughts are grouped in a section entitled *De la nécessité du Pari*. Of course, Pascal was laying his bet on the truth of Christianity. He said:

> I shall have far greater fear of deceiving myself [by not accepting it and then] finding that the Christian religion is true, than of not deceiving myself by believing that it is true.

13

This could be extended to any kind of faith, religious or non-religious. In summing up these thoughts of Pascal, Léon Brunschvigc wrote:

> In fact, for a man of honest faith and in possession of freedom of mind, the finite is annihilated by the infinite; present life, if one knows oneself exactly, is nothing, so that were it that a man was deceived in his hope, he will have nothing to regret; and in this lies the triumphant force of the argument about wager ...

In this connection, an argument put forward by Pascal is worthy of note. It is this: 'Mathematics, which is the rational science par excellence, does it not feel compelled to recognize the Infinite, whose nature, nevertheless, is inconceivable in reason?'

I shall repeat that this argument can be extended to my assumption. Let me next consider a serious implication of this assumption of mine.

The Teleological Corollary to my Cosmological Assumption

Having arrived at the conviction that the universe is an endless process and flow, I was bound further to assume that the flow had a direction, that it was advancing towards a goal; predetermined, or inchoate and immanent, I could not tell.

Yet the cosmological speculation of scientists rejects teleology, a purposive advance of the universe. They say that all that is happening in the universe is happening haphazardly, and there is no purpose to be discerned by reason. In my young days I believed in this kind of cosmology and was repelled by teleology. At that time I disliked the idea of creative evolution and the idea of emergences of new phenomena. This dislike extended equally to the notion of mutation of De Vries, and to the *élan vital* of Bergson, vitalism of Hans Driesch, and emergences of Lloyd Morgan. Yet at the end of life I have my bet on these ideas.

Now I certainly believe that there is purpose in evolution, or rather two purposes: one restricted to better adaptation to the circumstances of existence of all species; and the other extended to the creation of new forms of animal existence. I find it absurd to think that the evolution of species from the earthworm to man can be fortuitous. In that case, man's rationality, notion of progress, and perception of values would be reduced to self-deception. Can it be so?

I shall set down my idea of the universe (which is, of course, only an assumption incapable of being proved) in the words I employed in the second part of my autobiography:

> I believe that the universe is self-increate, and with all that it contains, namely, the values which are conventionally known as matter, mind, intellect, morality, spirituality, and so on, it is without end, although it might have had a beginning; the logical notion that everything which has a beginning must also have an end, not holding true in this case.
>
> I believe that in its flow the universe is purposive, and the purpose has been partly achieved, but for the greater part it remains to be fulfilled, and in this purpose are included all that the mind of man, yearning after perfection, has regarded as the highest values, e.g., beauty, goodness, righteousness, or holiness.
>
> I believe that the purpose is immanent in the universe, and not external to it, nor is it predestined as a complete idea, but that at every given moment the purpose is incomplete and infinitely potential.

(Thy Hand, Great Anarch! [1987] p. 955)

Perhaps in regard to the universe, what may be accepted as almost but not actually as the last word, was spoken by Ernest Renan in the reminiscences of his childhood and youth, which is generally considered to be his best literary production. I give my own translation, but an English translation of the book is available. What he says is equally against facile optimism and facile pessimism. The passage is as follows:

> Let us then, without worrying, leave the destiny of the planet to accomplish itself. Our lamentations will do nothing, our bad humour will be misplaced ... The universe does not know discouragement; it resumes those of its works that have miscarried; each check leaves it young, alert, full of illusions. Courage, Courage, Nature! Pursue like the deaf and blind starfish, which vegetates in the depths of the Ocean, your obscure toil of life; be dogged; repair the chain mail which has broken a thousand times, restart the drill to dig down to the attainable,

15

so as to reach the wells from which living waters will surge. Look forward, go on seeking the goal you have been missing since eternity; try to go through the imperceptible hole, through the opening which takes you to another sky. You have infinite space and infinite time for your experiments. When one has the right to deceive oneself with impunity one is always sure to succeed.

(Souvenirs d'Enfance et de Jeunesse,
28th impression, 1897 [first published 1883] p. xxi.

My Fundamental Assumption Regarding the Unification of Mankind

I have already said that I do not share the current belief that, given enough help, especially in money, all the different peoples on earth will become one human brotherhood, or as the Americans expect a worldwide American nation. I have to go deeper into the question.

I must say that, zoologically, there is justification for assuming that mankind is tending towards complete unity. That is to say, as a species of animal, it is the sole survivor in a zoological family and a zoological genus. This view was set forth in a book entitled *Uniqueness of Man,* written by Julian Huxley and published in 1941. In it he showed that the zoological evolution of the *Homo sapiens* had a very special feature of its own, unparalleled in the rest of the animal kingdom. While all other zoological families produced a number of genera and each genus produced a number of species, the species *Homo sapiens* became the only survivor in the family *Hominidae* and the genus *homo*. It is a genuine and stable species by all zoological critera. Thus man is united zoologically, and if that is so, why should he not become, in the next stage of evolution, united socially and culturally? If further human evolution were simply a continuation and extension of its bodily aspect, that is certainly a valid assumption. But will human evolution continue in the bodily line? That was the question which arose in my mind and I answered it differently.

It seemed to me that in the animal world zoological evolution had come to an end. Certainly, so far as history and archaeology

16

has been able to establish, no new animal species has appeared on earth after the emergence of man, and now the existence of man has been taken back millions of years from the older scientifically assumed date. So, if no new species has appeared in this very long period of time, why should there be a new one in future?

Faced with this wall before me, I passed beyond it by assuming that zoological evolution has been left behind by psychological evolution, through which new psychological species will appear. In mind, in their way they will be as authentic a species as the zoological. This is not as untenable an assumption as it might appear to be at first sight. Nobody thinks of denying that man shares many bodily and mental features with animals; say, with dogs, horses or monkeys. Yet man does not regard himself as the same animal as these.

Similarly, I have assumed that in some five hundred or thousand years a particular psychological species of man will find that he is not quite like other human psychological species, although he will also admit that there are common features. I am extending the pattern of animal evolution to human evolution in a spirit of philosophical analogy. Although others might not accept my view, I do not see why it should be dismissed as untenable. All new views are rejected when they are first put forward. There are people who even now do not accept evolution and remain attached to the old notion of simultaneous creation.

My Third Fundamental Assumption: Parallelism Between the Life-cycles of Individuals and Nations

I have come to believe that the individual's life-cycle is more or less closely repeated in the life-cycle of nations. That is to say, just as an individual human being is born, grows to manhood; reaches the peak of his achievement, creative or conservative; has after that a period of static stability at the achieved level; and then begins to lose vitality to pass through old age to death; so does the collective entity—nation. It is seen at the first stage as a distinct genetic group or, in any case, as an ethnic group of different genetic origins but united by a common culture in the anthropologist's sense, in which a common language is the most important element; then it develops both political power and cultural achievement in the historian's sense and acquires a strong group-consciousness with self-assertiveness; this results both in political and cultural expansion; after this comes a stable staticity; finally this nation loses vitality and goes down the sloping path of decline; in the finale a nation sometimes disappears from history, but sometimes also continues in a feeble and uncreative state of being, as distinct from a state of becoming; this, if not equivalent to the individual's death, is at least in its subanimation very much like that.

Now, if this assumption of mine is not accepted as valid the whole thesis of my book falls through. If it is not accepted even for the sake of argument, I shall not be able to make my story of the decline and fall of Western civilization convincing.

If a nation continues to exist as a human group in a devitalized state instead of disappearing, I regard it as a decadent society. This diagnosis is not a moral judgement at all; it is half a biological and half an historical one. Yet most people regard it as a moral condemnation, and if it is applied to them they glare and growl with raised hackles.

I do not and cannot understand this attitude. I am very old and have lost all my youthful appearance as well as a good deal of physical strength, but I do not feel ashamed of it. Nevertheless, there may be states in old age in which there would be shame. That would be, if an old man approached death not in his bed, full of years and honours, but in a brothel, suffering from delirium tremens and syphilis. Nations too, can reach in their old age a golden augustanism or an ignoble existence in a figurative brothel.

It is in the light of this assumption that I shall write about the decline of Western civilization and I shall have to be frank about which of these two final states the people who have inherited Western civilization are showing signs of drifting towards.

My Last Fundamental Assumption: On the Value of Opinion and Fashion

In regard to public opinion, I have come to the firm historical conclusion—which makes it something different from a mere

18

assumption—that opinion does not shape the course of historical events, but that it simply obeys historical trends. In other words, whoever or whatever creates historical trends also operates on the human mind to create opinions favourable to them, for no change can take place in human affairs without the pressure of opinion. But as all historical trends are unpredictable, so are somersaults of opinion.

To begin with, I shall illustrate that by considering political changes. I take the abandonment of India in 1947. Almost down to 1946, British politicians who were in authority declared that they could not foresee any time when British rule in India would come to an end. Under American pressure in 1942, the Cripps Mission was indeed sent to India to make a contingent declaration of giving India independence. But the Indian nationalist leaders, including Gandhi, did not take it seriously. Yet when at the beginning of 1947 the decision to leave India was taken and announced, it was regarded as a wise and statesmanlike step.

On their part, the Indian nationalist leaders showed equal inconsistency. They had shown an adamantine opposition to any partition of India, declaring that to accept it would be acceptance of the 'two-nation' theory. Yet in the space of only seven days in March 1947 they accepted the proposal made by the British government to partition India. This defied even the wildest calculation of probabilities.

To bring such mutations of opinion within the scope of rational understanding is futile. Opinion, like the wind, bloweth where it listeth; apparently so, but not really. It becomes intelligible as soon as the historical trend is taken into account.

Whatever that is, opinion will conform even when the historical trend is for the decline and fall of a nation. With this in mind, I wrote in the preface to my book *The Autobiography of an Unknown Indian*, published in 1951:

> Very few people seem to realize that nations stand in need of leadership in order to perish or rot away no less than to rise and achieve greatness. The exceptional men who play this evil role are mostly plebeians puissant in speech, who with plausible words mesmerize their fellows

to the agony of death or drive them like Gadarene swine over a precipice, after conjuring up a screen of black magic to hide the trap of death from the wretched herd. There have been too many of them in recent times, and there still are too many of them at the head of affairs in some of the leading countries for any naming of them to be necessary.

Although published in 1951, I actually wrote those words at the beginning of 1948, and I do not think that the nearly fifty years that have elapsed since then have invalidated them. In every change of opinion one sees the sequence of causality from the historical trend to the change of opinion, and not its converse.

I cannot dispute that in saying all this I am denying man's free-will, and succumbing to determinism. But that is a very special and restricted kind of determinism, a determinism operating in a part of the process of evolution, not in the whole. I am only saying that man cannot control his evolution or destiny, not that evolution itself in its wholeness is predetermined. On the contrary, that whole, so far from being predetermined, seems to be very much like groping towards an end, which a priori is undetermined, being alternations in a process of trial and error. This will come out clearly in a citation from Renan which I shall give later.

But there is determinism in one sense even in that unsure groping. The groping in this case is always obeying a pre-existent trend and can never go against it. This process is very much like a river flowing down to the sea with many windings, never in a straight course. At times the windings of a river seem even to drift away from the course to the sea. For instance, at Benares the Ganges swerves north instead of going along its normal south-eastern course. But it resumes its proper direction further down. Something like that on a smaller scale is seen in the Thames from Westminster Bridge to Blackfriars Bridge, so beautifully painted by Canaletto. Man's evolution seems to resemble that; that is to say, the final goal is determined, the river must reach a sea suggested by the trend but its course will be irregular.

I come, last of all, to fashions; in costumes specially. To relate them to climate and weather is only to take refuge in a commonplace; no kind of clothing is worn only for protection against heat or cold. If it were so, there would be uniformity of clothes within one climatic zone. But that is never the case, for even within one of these zones there are variations, at times very wide. All the features of any class of costumes cannot be re-related to the weather and climate. In what way can the ruff of the sixteenth century be connected with weather?

In one of his stories Kipling makes an English forest officer, living alone in a sub-Himalayan jungle, dress for dinner, 'because it had been his custom to do so to preserve his self-respect, but with the result that the stiff white shirt-front creaked with his regular breathing'. Again, what had the tight hose of the young men of the age of Renaissance to do with European climate and weather?

I need not labour such truisms. The truth about fashions is that they are invariably, in their conscious motivation at least, related to sexual life, and have the aim of arousing sexual desire. But the different ways of doing this cannot be explained rationally. Fashion is always sub-rational and the only way in which it can be justified by reason is to say that there is method even in madness.

But considering the question broadly, it can be said that fashions are meant to evoke sexual desire, and the manner of doing it varies according to the historical trend. An age of elegance creates elegant clothing. But vulgar ages will not only create vulgarity, but even persecute everything that is not vulgar.

To take the present age, in it what is obvious is that in its fashions one sees the dominance of the sexual desire which today is only less powerful than the greed for money. It is, however, seen in two forms: *haute couture* and *basse couture*. The *haute* is *outré* and the *basse* shabby. The sexual appeal in the *haute* is meretriciously sophisticated, in the *basse* it is crude. But both have the same aim. The fashionable clothes could be called a rapier of sensuality and the shabby a bludgeon. Both are equally effective.

From ancient Egypt and Mesopotamia, down to our own days fashions for women have obeyed the same urge, but according to the taste of a particular age. Since there is no such thing as 'taste' in the contemporary world there is no exhibition of taste in its specific meaning. What is seen everywhere one can explain only by repeating the popular saying: 'There is no accounting for taste.' I do not think I have to say anything more in regard to this fundamental assumption of mine.

Chapter 4

Of State of Mind

All that will be found in this book was in my mind in its final wording, before I thought I would set it down on paper. That last embodiment of my thoughts for others hardly makes any difference to my self-expression. It is only like printing a photographic negative on paper. The print can show nothing which is not in the negative.

Just then an event shed a wholly different light on what I was going to say. It was the sudden death of my wife on 17 September 1994. She had been a heart patient for over eight years, with other serious disabilities like arthritis. Over all that time I tried to prepare myself for the inevitable. That needed special effort. We had been married sixty-two years and during that period I had not, counting all absences, been separated from her for more than six or seven months. Also, I had not seen anyone dying before my eyes. I was absent at the death of all my relatives, paternal, maternal, and in-law. Yet I am the only survivor. Last of all, since my twenty-fifth year I had lost all belief in the survival of the human personality in an incorporeal form in an eternal world.

It was not that we did not discuss death at our advanced ages—hers eighty-five and mine ninety-seven. She used to say that she would prefer to go first, except for her worry about me. I said I would like to go first. But, of course, no choice was left to us. My friends give me the sensible consolation that as the survivor, she would have suffered more, not only from grief, but also from the compulsion to live alone. There would have been nobody to look after her, disabled as she was in many ways. That is perfectly true, but reason does not lessen feelings.

What happened to me, I can describe in the words of Sir Thomas Browne: 'The Night of Time far surpasseth the Day, and who knows when was the Equinox?' Equinox, of course, there never was for those who lived. It was for that reason that the Romans described dying as joining the majority and the way of life of the ancestors as the *mos maiorum*, the way of life of the 'majority'.

But the Night of Time descends only on surviving human beings, not on the Cosmos. The universe continues to exist in eternal light. Yet I as an individual can no longer see that light, though living. For me the Night of Time has descended on the lighted universe. That has made a radical change in my life. In my vocation as a writer I had always been an *engagé*, totally immersed and involved in the affairs of the world. But suddenly, I lost all interest in that world. How I now see the world I shall set down in the words of Robert Bridges:

> A man who rambling wide hath turn'd
> resting on some hill-top
> to view the plain he has left,
> and see'th it now out-spread
> mapp'd at his feet, a landscape
> so by beauty estranged
> he scarce wil ken familiar haunts,
> nor his home,
> maybe, where far it lieth
> small as a faded thought.

(*The Testament of Beauty*, 1930, p.1)

I am now seeing the world I have lived in and fought in exactly in the same way, perhaps, as I would see it today from an aeroplane. I no longer see it in three dimensions, I see it only like a map, with everything in its location.

What new light death sheds on individualism I shall describe in a later chapter of the book in which I shall consider man's true relationship with the Cosmos. Here I am only asking the reader to remember that my old world is now seen by me very brilliantly indeed, but also softly, with a new chiaroscuro.

PART TWO

Of Three Horsemen of the New Apocalypse

The First Horseman

A white horse: and he that sat on him had a bow: and a crown was given unto him; and he went forth conquering and to conquer.

INDIVIDUALISM (Contemporary)

The Second Horseman

Another horse *that was* red and *power* was given to him that sat thereon to take peace from the earth; and that they should kill one another; and there was given unto him a great sword.

NATIONALISM (Contemporary)

The Third Horseman

A black horse, and he that sat on him had a pair of balances in his hand.

And I heard a voice ... say, A measure of wheat for a penny, and three measures of barley for a penny; and *see* that thou hurt not the oil and the wine.

DEMOCRACY (Contemporary)

—The Revelation of St John the Divine, ch. 6 vv 2–6 as in the King James Bible.

I have omitted the Fourth Horseman, Death, because he puts an end to the roles of the first three. I have derived the images of the Three from an engraving of Albrecht Dürer in the British Museum.

Chapter 1

Of Individualism

History of the Word

The word 'individual', derived from mediaeval Latin, came into the English language with the Renaissance. Its first citation in the OED is from 1405. At that time it was an adjective, not a noun. Citations of later usage in this dictionary are from 1625.

Nonetheless, compared with 'individualism', 'individual' is an old word. Its derivative 'individualism' did not appear until the first half of the nineteenth century. The suffix '-ism' is derived from verbs formed with the suffix '-ize', and when found added to a stem it indicates belief in or behaviour in accordance with what *ism* stands for. The number of combinations with *ism* is formidable—say, from 'absolutism' to 'zionism', and in modern usage the combination is multiplying *ad libitum*, often pejoratively.

'Individualism' thus means not belief in the existence of the human individual, which needs no proof, but belief in the individual's supreme worth and importance, as well as in his right to act as he pleases.

The first citation of the word 'individualism' in the OED is from H. Reeve's English translation of the second part (Tomes 3 and 4) of Tocqueville's *Démocratie en Amérique*.

So it may be in France as well. The writer of the article on 'Individualism' in the latest (1972) version of the 14th edition of the *Encyclopaedia Britannica*, an American professor, says that the word was coined by Tocqueville. This is not correct, for Tocqueville himself wrote:

27

L'individualism est une expression récent qu'un idée nouvelle a fait naître. Nos pères ne connaissaient que l'égoisme.

[Individualism is a recent expression which has been brought into existence by a new idea. Our fathers knew only egoism.]

(De la Démocratie en Amérique, nrf edition, Gallimard, 1961, p. 105)

Tocqueville's own definition of egoism was: 'L'égoisme est un amour passioné et exagéré de soi-même, qui porte l'homme à ne rien rapporter qu'à lui seul et à se preferer à tout' (Egoism is a passionate and exaggerated love of oneself which makes a man connect everything to himself and prefer himself to all).

Individualism on the other hand was, according to Tocqueville, a wholly different thing. As he put it:

L' individualisme est un sentiment réfléchi et paisible qui dispose chaque citoyen à s'isoler de la masse de ses semblables et à se retirer à l'écart avec sa famille et ses amis de sorte que, aprés, a s'être ainsi crée une petite société à son usage, il abandonne volontiers la grande société à elle-même.

[Individualism is a deliberate and calm feeling which disposes every citizen to isolate himself from the mass of people like him, and to live apart with his family and friends in a manner so that after creating a small society for his own use he voluntarily leaves the society at large to itself.]

What does Individualism Mean?

As the word appears first in English in Reeve's translation of the second part of Tocqueville's *Democracy in America,* published in 1842, it would be proper at the outset to give his conception of what individualism stood for. The definition just quoted embodies that succinctly, but Tocqueville considered the American practice of individualism in its different aspects and applications in eleven chapters in Part II of the second half of his work (pp. 105–39 of the nrf edition).

The following summary may be regarded as Tocqueville's basic description of individualism in the United States:

In democratic societies new families spring up necessarily from nothing, and those which remain undergo change; the woof of time is severed every moment, and the vestiges of past generations disappear. Therefore people easily forget those who have preceded them, and acquire no idea of those who will follow them. The nearest are the only ones who interest them.

Thus it will be seen that Tocqueville's description of individualism as understood and practised by Americans simply means that an individual has the right to pursue self-interest in the form of acquisition of money and fulfilment of all desires, good or bad, also amenities of life, without external constraints. He also pointed out how this self-centred preoccupation was modified in the United States by other considerations, which emanated from a feeling that for the pursuit of self-interest to remain unimpeded it must also be accompanied by a liberality to the self-interest of other individuals. It was this feeling which made the American plutocrats like Carnegie and Rockefeller create munificent endowments for promoting knowledge. It was self-interest pursued in an enlightened and intelligent manner.

It is easy to discover where this kind of individualism came from. The principle was embodied in a short sentence of the Declaration of Independence: 'We hold these truths to be self-evident ... that they [all men] are endowed by their Creator with certain inalienable Rights, that among them are Life, Liberty and the pursuit of Happiness' (adopted 4 July 1776).

Didacticism is always unrealistic and here is no exception. If this unqualified assertion were true, the same Creator would not have subjected man to death which annuls all these inalienable Rights of his without any reference to his wishes. On the contrary, the truth which is self-evident is contained in the saying of Victor Hugo: 'All men are under a sentence of death, with only indefinite reprieves.'

I shall deal with the issue which this pronouncement raises, i.e. the relationship between individualism and death, in its proper place. In the meanwhile, I shall take stock of the meanings which dictionaries give to the word 'individualism'.

Dictionaries on 'Individualism'

I shall quote only the *Oxford English Dictionary* (*OED*) and the edition of the *Webster International,* as mentioned in the preface to this book. For my purpose their definitions will be sufficient.

The *OED* gives five senses to the word, the first of which is identical with Tocqueville's definition of individualism in the United States: 'A mode of life in which the individual pursues his own ends or follows out his own ideas.' However, the *OED* differs from Tocqueville in equating this kind of individualism with egoism.

The second meaning given to the word in the *OED* is put in the following words: 'The social theory which advocates the free and independent action of the individual, as opposed to communistic method of organization and State interference.'

The third meaning in the *OED* is characterized as 'metaphysical' and is given as 'the doctrine that an individual is a self-determined whole, and that any larger whole is merely an aggregate of the individuals, which if they act on each other at all, do so externally.'

The fourth and fifth meanings of the *OED* are identical with 'individuality', which is a loose, if not incorrect application of the word.

None of the meanings given by the *OED* correspond to the generally current and accepted meaning today.

Let me now turn to the meanings in the *Webster International.* The first of these is synonymous with individuality; the second corresponds to Tocqueville's definition of individualism in America.

The third and fourth meanings in this dictionary are inter-related. The third is given as 'the doctrine or practice which holds that the chief end of society is the promotion of individual welfare ... that society exists for the sake of its individual members'.

The fourth meaning is: 'a theory or policy having primary regard for individual rights, specf. one maintaining the political and economic independence of the individual.'

In these two senses 'individualism' is almost identical with Bentham's Utilitarianism and the economic doctrine of *laissez faire*.

The fifth sense in *Webster* is the biological, of no significance except in biology.

The sixth sense given by *Webster* is called ethical, viz. 'the doctrine which says that the interest of the individual should be paramount in the determination of conduct—ethical egoism'.

The seventh sence in the dictionary is called philosophical and is explained as follows: 'The self is the only knowable existence: egoism.'

Thus I find that not *one* of the many meanings given to the word by the two dictionaries refers to the individual's life and functioning, which is the main issue in this book. They are all concerned not with the individual *per se*, but with his relations with the state or society in which he lives. All the meanings leave the all-important question unanswered: What then is individualism in itself, i.e. in its function in the individual's own life and activities?

One Powerful Assertion of the Individual's Right

I have failed to find a clear answer, let alone a detailed, systematized answer to the question. But I have found a very emphatic declaration of the individual's right to be himself and assert himself. It is in a letter of Alexander Herzen, the revolutionary Russian thinker, to Giuseppe Mazzini, written on 13 September 1850. I quote it from an English translation given by Sir Isaiah Berlin in his book *Russian Thinkers* (Hogarth Press, London, 1978, p.82.):

> Since the age of thirteen ... I have served one idea, marched under one banner—war against all imposed authority—against every kind of deprivation of freedom, in the name of the absolute independence of the individual. I should like to go on with my little guerilla war like a real Cossack.

This is an extreme assertion of individualism which has never been successfully put into effect in any country or in any age. On the other hand, in every country and in every age the individual's freedom has been restricted, first by the state or society, and secondly by his own moral scruples.

It is not difficult to explain why Herzen made such a claim for the individual's liberty of thought and action, which on the face of it seems so irresponsible. He was not a young man then, with youth's penchant for ruthless statements. He was thirty-eight and mature. The reason is to be found in the political and intellectual situation in Europe in the middle of the nineteenth century.

But before I describe that, I have to emphasize that beyond making the claim, Herzen never spoke or wrote about the purpose for which he wanted individual liberty.

Sir Isaiah Berlin in his essays on Herzen can only say that to Herzen the goal of life was life itself and to sacrifice the present to some vague future was a delusion, a sacrifice of the flesh and blood of living human beings on the altar of idealized abstractions.

Sir Isaiah Berlin cites two statements made by Herzen himself on this question. The first of them is this:

> We think the purpose of the child is to grow up because it does grow up. But its purpose is to play, to enjoy itself, to be a child. If we merely look to the end of the process, the purpose of all life is death.

The second one is this:

> Why is liberty valuable? Because it is an end in itself, because it is what it is. To bring it as a sacrifice to something else is simply to perform an act of human sacrifice.

It is clear that Herzen saw the bearing of death on individualism, but would not admit its relevance. The life which Herzen had resolved to live was the unexamined life which Plato said (or, more accurately, put in the mouth of Socrates) was not worth living. *Ó de ánexétastos Bi'os o'u Biotòs anthrópo.*

Authoritarianism in Europe from 1815 to 1870

Herzen's extreme and to all appearances irresponsible assertion about the individual's right would, however, become perfectly intelligible in the light of his own experiences. He was born in 1812, and as he grew up he saw authoritarianism not only becoming more absolute but being erected into a system of international relations by the Congress of Vienna and its sequels. In respect of government its creators were Metternich and Castlereagh, and its doctrinal justification came from two French political thinkers, De Bonald and Joseph de Maître.

A breach in this system was indeed made by the July (1830) Revolution in France, which created a more or less liberal bourgeois political regime. But it was not a militant regime. On the contrary, it had a peaceful coexistence with the absolutist regimes. The more truly revolutionary outbreak followed in 1832, but it was ruthlessly suppressed. Victor Hugo described it in his *Les Miserables*.

The really serious revolt against absolutism in Europe came in 1848, and at first it seemed to succeed. But it was crushed with severity. What followed were even more absolute regimes, specially in Austria–Hungary and Russia, under Emperor Francis-Joseph and Czar Nicolas I, respectively. Even in France a new authoritarian regime, the Second Empire of Napoleon III, emerged. In Prussia, too, under Bismarck's direction, there was an authoritarian regime in spirit, although not in constitutional form.

Herzen had to see the dominance of all these enemies of individualism, and he died in Paris on 21 January 1870. He did not see the overthrow of Napoleon III. Before that, however, he must have been somewhat heartened on seeing some relaxation of authoritarianism in Russia with the accession of Alexander II towards the end of the Crimean War, on 2 March 1855. The military failure in that war created a surge of liberalism and it made all thinking Russians feel the necessity of reform in all branches of government. This feeling found its most notable expression in the emancipation of the serfs decreed on 3 March 1861.

But this 'Indian Summer' of liberalism in Russia was brought to an end by the assassination of Alexander II by anarchists in 1881. What followed was the rigorous autocracy of Alexander III, the doctrinal advocate of which was the famous Russian conservative thinker, Pobedonostsev (1827–1907).

He had a deep hatred and fear of democratic or even constitutional government, freedom of the press, and religious freedom. He was largely responsible for the repression of all liberal thinkers and activists during the reign of Alexander III. All Russian revolutionists regarded him as the symbol of the old regime and called him the Grand Inquisitor.

The authoritarianism preached by him was inherited by Nicolas II in a blind and unreflective form, which therefore became wholly stolid. Although challenged by revolutionary movements from 1905, its de facto power remained intact till it was destroyed by the revolutions of 1917. To me, a young student then, the British government in India appeared to be an exact replica of the czarist regime and showed the same attitude towards the Indian nationalist movement. Both were unintelligent and effete, but both possessed the grip of the dead hand.

Republican France and the Anti-Democratic Ideology

Even in France, liberalism as a doctrine was not unchallenged. The downfall of the Second Empire did indeed bring into existence the largest lasting republic in France, the third, but internally it was unstable, as was seen in the rapid succession of ministries from 1871 to 1914. In no other parliamentary regime was such a spectacle seen. This internal disequilibrium in republican France was brilliantly exposed by Bodley in his famous book.

The instability in administration was accompained by an ideological movement which was strongly anti-democractic, and the two subsisted side by side. Before I describe this paradox I have however to deal with a connected theoretical question, namely the relationship between the idea of liberty and the idea of individualism.

The best-known and most elaborate discussion of this relationship is to be found in John Stuart Mill's book on *Liberty*, published in 1859. But I have come upon an equally acute although more succinct analysis in a book first published in 1856 but in its final text in 1858. It is Alexis de Tocqueville's *L'Ancien Régime et la Révolution*. I would stress the importance of the relationship, because individualism cannot function without liberty and liberty cannot have any raison-d'être without individuals to take advantage of it. Equality is not so closely related to individualism. Still, it is also necessary for its widest exercise, since without equality of opportunity for all, individualism cannot be the right of the largest possible number of individuals.

Now, liberty is neither political and social independence nor freedom from external restraint. Liberty, strictly interpreted, means the right of individuals to do what they wish to do or to enjoy as an asset or privilege. I shall now cite Tocqueville's exposition of the condition of liberty in my translation from the French:

> The notion of liberty can appear in the human mind in two different forms. It can be seen (1) as the exercise of a common right or (2) as the enjoyment of a privilege.
>
> To wish to remain free for all actions or some of them, not at all because all men have a general right to be independent, but because a person by himself has a special right to remain independent; such was the manner in which liberty was understood in the Middle Ages, and as such it has always been understood in aristocratic societies, in which circumstances are very inequal and in which the human mind, having once acquired the habit of having privileges, end by adding to the number of them, also to the acquisition of all the good things of the world. ...This aristocratic notion of liberty produces in those who inherit it, an exalted sentiment of their worth as individuals, a passionate desire for independence. It gives energy and also a singular power to egoism. As understood by individuals, it has often led men to the most extraordinary actions; when adopted by a whole people it has created the greatest nations that have ever existed.

Of such nations, Tocqueville gives the example of the Romans. This is illustrated by Virgil's admonition to the Romans: *'Tu regere imperio populos, Romane, memento Hae erunt tibi artes'* (O Romans, remember that yours is the role to exercise domination over peoples. In this lie your arts). The British from the very first regarded their rule in India in the same light.

Tocqueville gives next the notion of liberty as exercised in democratic societies:

> According to modern and democratic notions of liberty, which I presume to regard as correct, it means that every human being who can be assumed to have received from Nature the necessary lights to conduct himself, brings to himself with his birth an equal and unprescriptable

right to live according to his wishes, independently of his likes in respect of all that concerns only himself, and also to regulate his own destiny.

Tocqueville continues:

> As soon as this notion of liberty has penetrated deeply into the consciousness of a people and become firmly established among them, absolute power is no longer anything but a material fact, only a passing accident, because when everyone has an absolute right over oneself, it follows that a sovereign will can emanate only from the united will of all. From thence, obedience to authority loses moral validity and there is no middle course between the virile and proud virtue of a citizen on the one hand and the low complaisance of a slave on the other.
>
> In proportion as social ranks become equal in a people this notion of liberty tends to prevail.

An important point to note is that in this exposition of liberty the reference to 'necessary lights from Nature' suggests an approximation to the *Ius Naturae* of old jurisprudence.

Tocqueville makes an additional observation which makes the connection between liberty and individualism more explicit. I quote the key passage :

> The idea that each individual, and by extension each people, has the right to control his own or their acts—this idea still obscure, partially defined and ill-formulated, instils itself little by little into all minds. It stops formally at theory in enlightened classes; it reaches, by a sort of instinct, the entire people. It results in a new and more impulsive movement towards liberty ... it becomes a reasoned-out and systematized option.

Authoritarianism as Fact and in Theory in Europe from 1870 to 1914

Authoritarianism in the religious sphere asserted itself *as fact* even before the collapse of the Second Empire in France. That was seen in the formal declaration of papal infallibility by the Vatican Council of 1870, on 18 July, one day before the outbreak of the Franco-Prussian War.

It deprived all sincere Catholics of the right to private opinion on Christian beliefs, and they were bound to obey the Council's decision, which may be summarized as follows:

(i) The Roman Pontiff, when speaking *ex cathedra*, i.e. in discharge of the office of Pastor and Doctor of all Christians, is possessed of infallibility;

(ii) Therefore such definitions of the Roman Pontiff are unalterable in themselves, and not by the consensus of the Church.

But it would be unfair to single out the Catholic Church for intolerance. The Anglican Church was not a whit less so. In 1849 J.A. Froude, the historian, had to see his book, *Nemesis of Faith*, burnt at his college, Exeter, at Oxford, and also to lose his fellowship. Even his father, an archdeacon, stopped the allowance he gave to his son. The university required any fellow suspected of unorthodoxy to reassert his acceptance of the Thirty-nine Articles, which imposed royal authority on the Anglican Church in all matters except doctrine.

In fact, all religions, so long as they remain living, remain intolerant. There is no such religion as a permissive religion. Heresy-hunting is natural for all living religions. When a religion ceases to be intolerant it ceases to be religion in the true sense of the word. In addition if it becomes liberal or latitudinarian it becomes merely religious opinion.

It must not be assumed that the right of 'Private Judgement' claimed by Protestantism admitted the individual's right to decide what is orthodoxy; it only meant that an individual Christian had the right to go to the scriptures for a correct idea of Christianity, and was not bound to accept tradition or a denominational interpretation of it.

Besides Christianity, Islam was and remains still more intolerant. It denies the right of all non-Muslims even to live unless they are 'people of the Book', i.e. Jews or Christians, *Dhimmis* as they were called. They could buy their life by paying a special tax. Nowadays a very incorrect phrase 'Islamic Fundamentalists' has become current. There is no such thing. A Muslim is either a 'Fundamentalist' or not a Muslim at all.

Hinduism is also intolerant in its particular way. It has no creed, and so there is no doctrinal heresy in it. A Hindu is born a Hindu, and cannot become a Hindu otherwise. Such a Hindu may hold any dogma and still remain a Hindu, provided he accepts (i) the revealed character of the Vedas (without, of course, any knowledge of them) and (ii) observes every Hindu social taboo. If he disregards any of the latter he is put outside the pale, and no Hindu will even sweep his house or wash his clothes. The cruelty of Hindu society in exercising this social coercion was not less blatant than that of the Inquisition. Modern Hindu orthodoxy in its true form knew neither justice nor compassion.

I shall now consider authoritarianism in Europe in its political aspect. It appeared in a new form with the proclamation of the German Empire at Versailles on 18 January 1871. The great German historians Treitscnke and Sybel became propagandists of the Prussian form of political authoritarianism.

Ideologically, however, the emergence of a doctrine of authoritarianism was far more important. And it appeard in republican France. Its first and most influential exponent was the great doctrinaire French intellectual, H. Taine. The horror of the Commune produced in him a strong revulsion for democracy and he gave expression to it in his historical works on the Ancient Regime and the Revolution. Although afterwards Aulard pointed out the shortcomings of his method of research, at the time there was no one to oppose his ideas with equal prestige and literary competence. He coined the dictum: 'Ten thousand ignorances do not constitute a wise man.' This was, of course, an extension of the mathematical axiom that zeroes add up only to zeroes. Taken as a class, the intellectuals of France showed a pronounced anti-democratic bias. Even as late as 1910 or thereabouts Émile Faguet published a book entitled *The Cult of Incompetence*, which was his description of the working of democracy.

But, both doctrinally and as an organized body of political propagandists for it, the anti-democratic thought found its most powerful exponents in a group of distinguished French writers who banded themselves under the slogan, L'Action Française. The doctrinaire leader of the band was Charles Maurras. He preached royalism and also the dogma of *nationalism intégrale.* In respect of nationalism, another writer, Maurice Barrès was an influential colleague of his.

I read the anti-democratic book of Maurras, *L'Avenir de l'Intelligence,* published in 1904, in early life and was very deeply impressed by it. I shall quote a passage from it when I deal with democracy. After the advent of Hitler the authoritarianism of Maurras led him to support Nazism during World War II. For this, after the Allied victory, Maurras was tried for treason and condemned to life imprisonment. His name was struck off from its records by the French Academy. But all that does not affect his literary standing, nor the cogency of his anti-democratic argument. On the practical side, Maurras had as colleague a very effective propagandist, Léon Daudet, the son of Alphonse Daudet.

I shall cite their opinions as quoted by Julien Benda in his famous book, *La Trahison des Clercs,* published in 1927. Here is a significant statement:

... travaille a la grandeur de la nation, sans qu'aucune place soit laisse aux volontes pariculierews.

On les a vus persuadés que les États ne sont forts qu'autant qu'ils sont autoritaires, faire l'apologie des régimes autocratiques, du gouvernement par l'arbitraire, par la raison d'État, des religions qui enseignent la soumission aveugle à une autorité, et n'avoir pas assez d'anathèmes pour les institutions à la base de liberté et de discussion; la flétrissure du liberalism, notamment par l'immease majorité des hommes de lettres actuel, est une des choses de ce temps qui étonnere le plus l'histoire, surtout de la part d'hommés de lettres français.

On les a vus les veux toujours fixés sur l'État fort, exalter l'État discipliné à la prussienne, ou chacun a son poste, et sous les ordres d'en haut, travaille à la grandeur de la nation, sans qu'aucune place soit laissé aux volontés particulières.

[They have been seen to be persuaded that States are powerful in proportion as they are authoritarian; to offer any apology for autocratic regimes, for arbitrary government by raison d'etat, for those religions which teach blind submission to authority, not to have enough anathemas for institutions based on liberty and on discussion; withering contempt for liberalism specially by contemporary intellectuals is wrong. It is one of those features of our age which will astonish history most, above all, French men of letters.

They have been seen to have their eyes always fixed on the powerful State, to exalt the State disciplined in the Prussian manner, in which everyone is at his post, under orders from above, works for the greatness of the nation without leaving any room for individual wills.]

I might add, incidentally, that this also was the principle on which the British government in India was run, and which was the reason for its success. As Kipling put it:

> They obey, the sergeant his lieutenant, and the lieutenant his captain, and the captain his major, and the major his colonel, and the colonel his brigadier, and the brigadier his general, who obeys the Viceroy, who is the servant of the Empress.

And what is most wonderful is that the present rulers of India also want to run their government on the same principle.

The reference to Prussian discipline in the above passage may be elaborated upon by an amplification of it given by Fustel de Coulanges, the great French historian of institutions. It runs as follows:

> The German historians demand that their nation be intoxicated by the personality of their nation even in its barbarism; similarly, the French moralists are not contented simply with that. They wish that their compatriots should accept that their 'national determinism' in its indivisible totality, with its injustice as its wisdom, with fanaticism as its clarities, with its pettiness as its greatness.

Maurras says: 'Good or bad, our tastes are ours, and it is praiseworthy for us to accept ourselves as the sole judge and model for our life' (*La Trahison des Clercs*, pp. 103–4).

I shall now quote a few direct pronouncements from Maurras and Barrès:

Maurras:

(a) La politique determine la morale.

[Politics determines what is moral.]

(b) Tout ce qui est bien du point de vue politique est bien, et je ne sais pas d'autrecriterium du bien.

[All that is good from the political point of view is good, and I do not know any other criterion of good.]

Maurras on Compassion:

(c) Cette pitie denatureux a degrade l'amour. Il s'est nommde nomme la charite; chacun s'est cru dignede lui. Les sots, les faibles, les infirmes ont rocu sa rosee. De nuit en nuit s'est entendu la semence de ce fleau. Elle remplit les solitudes. En quelque Elle conquirt la terre. Elle remplit les solitudes. En quelque contree que ce soit, on ne pas marcher un seul un sel sans recontrer ce visage fletrie au geste mediocre, mu du siple desir de prlonger sa vue honteuse.

[This denatured pity has degraded love. It calls itself charity. Everyone thinks that he is worthy of it. Idiots, weaklings, incapables have received its dewdrop. From night to night has this been seen—the sowing of this plague. It is conquering the world. It fills up the solitudes. Whichever country one may be in, one cannot be in it for a single day without coming upon its pallid visage, with its trivial motive of prolonging its shameful existence.]

(*Action Française,* Tome IV p. 569,
cited by Benda in his book, p. 174)

Barrès:

(a) Toutes les questions doivent etre résolues par rapport a la France.

[All questions must be resolved in their connection with France.]

(b) Que me parlez-vous de justice d'humanité? Qu'est-ce J'aime moi? Quelques tableux en Europe et quelques cimitières.

[Do not talk to me of justice among mankind. What do I love myself? A few paintings in Europe and a few graveyards.]

(c) C'est le role des maîtres de justifier les habitude et prejugé's qui sont ceux de la France, de manière à preparer pour le mieux nos enfants à prendre leur rang dans la procession nationale.

[It is the role of the masters to justify their habits and the prejudices which are those of France, and in a manner so that they may better take their rank in the national procession.]

I do not think I have to multiply such citations. Those I have given should be enough to demonstrate the strength and passion behind this nationalistic authoritarianism.

What made it even more powerful was the fact that virtually the entire intellectual élite of France was behind this kind of authoritarianism, some directly, some at second-hand by the implication of their writings.

Even Taine, Bergson, Émile Faguet, Paul Clandel could be assumed to have fostered authoritarianism in thinking. Their distrust in democracy was created by the excesses of the insurrection of the Paris Commune.

World War I and Authoritarianism

The ideological campaign begun by L'Action Française continued almost till the outbreak of World War I. Its impact on practical politics was seen in the riots in Paris over the Stavisky affair in 1934. But the rest of political life, as seen in government liberalism and parliamentarism, was certainly normal.

So, when World War I broke out in August 1914, at once for propaganda reasons it was given an ideological character. It was not, of course, an ideological war in its real character, but a war of *realpolitik* as well as power politics, primarily between Britain and Germany, but in formal international character a conflict between the Triple Entente and the Triple Alliance, the first being an association among Britain, France and Russia; and the second among Germany, Austria and Italy. The issue between the two sides was (i) domination of Europe resulting in an overthrow of balance of power, which was the keystone of British foreign policy; (ii) colonial expansion; and (iii) the right of Germany to be a world power, asserted under this slogan: 'Germany's place in the sun.'

Nonetheless, the war from the beginning was invested with an aura or camouflage of ideology. Even at its very beginning, I read as a young university student a book which was a collection of articles written by the leading English sociologist Hobhouse, in which he said that the War was made inevitable by the steady evolution of Germany towards authoritarianism and progressive abandonment of the basic principles of European civilization.

The idea that the war was ideological was confirmed by the enunciation of his form as 'Fourteen Points' by President Wilson on 8 January 1918. These enunciated the principles on which every question of international relation had been raised by the War. In a later speech President Wilson made explicit his conception of the ends envisaged by these points. The most important of these was: 'The destruction of every arbitrary power anywhere that can separately, secretly, and of its single choice disturb the peace of the world.'

Germany surrendered on the basis of the Fourteen Points accepted without reservation. But the long-term consequences were very different.

The final peace settlement imposed by the Versailles Conference and its ancillaries seemed, on the face of it, to be a victory for liberalism and freedom. But what it actually led to within a few years was the emergence of three of the most evil authoritarian political regimes seen in history, the Soviet regime in Russia, the Fascist in Italy, and the Nazi in Germany.

The war between freedom and autocracy had to be fought over again from 1939 to 1945, which, though a formal military victory for freedom, has had fatal consequences for Western civilization and European influence in the world.

The Impact of the War on the Conception of Individualism

I have given this very lengthy account of the domination of authoritarian doctrines in Europe in order to explain why individualism has become a force driving the process of the decline of Western civilization. The degradation of the individual was an extreme reaction to the evil authoritarianism that brought about the War.

The present notion of individualism is just unrestrained self-indulgence, more especially in regard to money and sexual relations. It is primarily an American product, but it has spread to all countries of the world, and is continuing to spread relentlessly. So it is bound to be destructive of civilization.

My View of Individualism

So, it seems that if one is to arrive at a true and *positive* conception of individualism, one must begin the quest from scratch, from a clean state—*tabula rasa.*

I was driven to do so by the time I was approaching the age of fifty, and set down an adumbration of it in the concluding lines of my *Autobiography of an Unknown Indian.* The passage in question was actually written in January 1948. The relevant part of it runs as follows:

> But in the last five or six years, through another miracle, I have been enabled to put an end to the duality (between the individual and the universe as asserted by religion). I have come to see that I and the universe are inseparable because I am only a particle of the universe and remain that in every manifestation of my existence, intellectual, moral and spiritual, as well as physical.

The Ambassador of Switzerland in India, who was a theologian, told me that these words alone showed that I could not be a Christian.

I have now fully developed my concept of individualism, and shall try to set it down as clearly as I can. I do not know whether anyone else has put forward such a view. So far as I know, no one has. What follows will be a summary of my view. But as the concept is many-sided, even the summary will be somewhat lengthy.

My basic hypothesis is that man is a part of the universe, being consubstantial with it, that is to say, being a particle of the eternal, flowing energy that the universe is, only limited in quantity and restricted to a short span of existence. In short, man is a microcosm in a macrocosm, comparable to an electrical battery.

But he does not stand in direct relation to the universe as the larger entity; his nexus to it is through another unit in it—which might be regarded, on account of the difference in size, as a microcosm in a macrocosm. This is the earth in which man lives.

This raises an insoluble question: Why should such a living being be able to formulate a rational and comprehensive view of the nature of the universe?

This was perceived by a great French moralist, Vauvenargues, who died at the early age of thirty-three on 28 May 1747. He wrote (Maxim No. 202 in the collection of his maxims):

> Un atome presque invisible, qu'on apelle l'homme, qui ranpe sur la face de la terre, et qui ne dure an'un jour, embrasse en quelque sorte d'un coup d'oeil le spectacle de l'univers dans tous les ages.

> [An almost invisible atom called man which rampages over the face of the earth and which exists for a day, brings to a certain extent within its *coup d'oeil* the universe in all its duration.]

The moral of this paradoxical fall is that neither size nor numbers count; what does count is quality, whose power seems to increase in proportion to the reduction in size.

So, when legitimately considered, this status of man does not justify his arrogance, but his proper status as an agent of the universe. This statement may be elaborated as follows: That the individual is made to work by the universe as its agent in the interest of the Cosmos for a work dictated by the Cosmos.

What is this work? It is manifold and has many aspects. In its primary aspect man's functioning is zoological, like any other animal's: to continue the existence of the human species. This work is involuntary.

It is only recently, by a total perversion of its real nature, that the physical act of sexual intercourse has been represented simply as a means of giving men pleasure without reference to procreation.

No more false and perverted view of sexual congress can be conceived of rationally. It is based on a false view of the feeling called pleasure and regarding pleasure as an end in itself, not as the means to an end—which in the case of sexual intercourse is procreation and bringing up children. Both are such onerous burdens that neither men nor women would take them up without a compensation in pleasure.

The corollary to this view of sexual congress is that contraception is a revolt against biology and therefore has also to be regarded as a repudiation of ethics. I remember how in my young days I angrily rejected the campaign of Marie Stopes. Although in our age, contraception has come to be regarded as a demographic necessity, I do not accept that.

I believe that individualism can be understood only in the light of man's life on earth, but in order to do so I must get round the religious view of it. That is totally opposed to the biological view.

The Religious View of Man's Life

All religions have represented death, which puts an end to man's existence on earth, as unimportant. They assert that man does not really belong to the earth. He is only a sojourner in it, coming into it from an eternal world and going back to that world with death.

It is not simply uneducated and credulous people who have held this view. So far as the history of man's mental life is known, this view of man's life on earth has been accepted as the truth about it. It has been so with men whose intellectual standing cannot be questioned. To give only one example, Wordsworth wrote:

> Our birth is but a sleep and a forgetting.
> The soul that rises with us, our life's Star,
> Hath had elsewhere its setting ...
> And cometh from afar ...
>
> *(Ode on the Intimations of Immortality)*

Tagore, the greatest poet India has produced, said in one of his songs: 'Death tells us "I only ply the boat of life".'

Even Walter Pater, who was suspected by the orthodox at Oxford of being a hedonist and a Cyreniastist, left on the cross of his grave the inscription, as I have myself seen: '*In Te, Domine, Speravi*' (In Thee, O Lord, I put my trust).

In this enumeration, I am leaving out men of religion, for example St Augustine, St Thomas Aquinas, Pascal. They could not have been men of religion unless they accepted the basic assumption of all religions regarding death.

In this respect, Pascal's position is particularly significant, for he was as great a scientist as he was a man of faith. But he drew an uncrossable barrier between the 'order of faith' and the 'order of the intellect' by saying: 'La distance infinie des corps aux esprit figure la distance infiniment, plus infinie des esprit à la charité, car elle est surnaturel.' (*Pensée*, No. 793).

Religion has gone further in its view of human life on earth. All religions, especially Christianity, have considered the world to be an evil place, in which man is every moment not only tempted but compelled to fall into evil ways unless protected by God's gift of grace. I give the Christian view of the world by quoting from the New Testament. In I St John (v.16), one reads these resounding words: 'For all that *is* in the World, the lust of the flesh, and the lust of the eyes, and the pride of life, is not of the Father, but is of the World.'

Therefore, in the Anglican Church, a boy when seeking confirmation as a Christian is made to answer a question as to what his godfather and godmother have done for him and he is required to answer: 'They did promise and vow...that I should renounce the devil and all his works, the pomps and vanity of this wicked world...'

But Christian preachers did not answer the question: If the world and life in it is such, why does God send man into this world, to have an intermezzo, which has no relationship to his real, eternal life. So, religion leaves us in the same uncertainty about man's life in the world and individuality as intellectual inquiry so far seen has done.

The religious view of life is anti-biological. Indeed, all religions in their basic stand revolt against biology.

So, I shall now put forward my view of death and its relationship to individualism.

47

The Individual and Death

The individual's life-cycle is predetermined by biology. It is at first growth, from birth to about middle-age, and then a gradual but unchecked decline, ending in death. Since a human being is basically an animal like all other animals, his existence is bound to be confined within the limits of animal life. Nothing else is established by observation.

This observable existence has, so to speak, an obverse and a reverse. These terms would lead one to expect static images. This precisely is *not* the case. The sides present moving pictures.

The obverse is the only side accessible to the organs of sense; the reverse remains inaccessible to the senses and is therefore ignored by the great majority of men. Nonetheless, it is as much a part of human life as the pictures on the obverse.

Figuratively, this ignored aspect of human existence may be compared to living in an immense palace, far larger than the Escorial or the Kremlin. It has radial aisles running from all directions to a round, central hall, in which stands a mysterious veiled figure; it has the capacity to face at the same time all the aisles down which individuals are marching irresistibly towards it.

But it never allows the marching files to see its face until one individual comes close to it. Then it whisks aside the veil and clasps the individual to its bosom. He sees the face, but he cannot tell what it is like—the face of the Gorgon Medusa, of Venus de Milo, or for that matter of La Notte of Michelangelo? For he passes into:

> The undiscover'd country
> from whose bourn
> No traveller returns.

But it is this very biological life-cycle of human life which is dismissed by all religions. No religion admits that man is an animal; all religions regard him as a special creation. If, however, the biological view of human life is admitted to be true, then one persistent moralizing on death has to be rejected. Throughout the ages wise men have moralized on the vanity of fame, which, they proclaim, is reduced to a hollow mockery by death.

Take, for instance, Pascal's frightening judgement: 'The last act is tragic (*sanglant*) however fine the comedy may be in all the rest: at last they throw earth on the head, and there we are for ever' (*Pensée*, No. 210).

Consider next Thomas Gray's famous stanza:

The boast of heraldry, the pomp of power,
And all that beauty, all that wealth e'er gave,
Awaits alike the inevitable hour—
The paths of glory lead but to the grave.

And, finally, James Shirley's stern warning:

The garlands wither on your brow;
Then boast no more your mighty deeds
Upon death's purple altar now
See where the Victor–Victim bleeds.
Your heads must come
To the cold tomb.

All this dismissal of fame only reiterates the oldest lament of disillusionment: *Vanitas vanitatum, Omnia vanitas*—Vanity of vanities, all is vanity. All these combinations, explicit or implicit, are magnificently phrased. On the face of it, all are true. But are they really?

The earth that was thrown on the head of Pascal has not buried his fame; Gray's *Elegy* is still read and was read by the present writer as a boy in rustic East Bengal; Shirley's garland has not, even in four centuries, withered on his brow.

This seems to give a new significance to fame. It would seem that fame is not an exclusive possession of the individual who earns it in his lifetime by his achievement; it is not a 'freehold' but belongs to him only as a life-interest. So, on his death, it reverts to the giver, the Cosmos, which gave it to him with a definite purpose of its own.

It is easy to discover that purpose. If the creative evolution of the Cosmos is to continue and, in addition, if what is created is to retain its value and influence, successive generations of men have to be compelled to remain in touch with those achievements. This requires labour, which no human being undertakes without some extraneous compulsion, without, so to speak, an 'assisted take-off'. That is provided by the fame of the individuals. To mention only one kind of achievement, would anybody have read Plato, Shakespeare or Goethe without the pressure exerted by their fame? That is the reason why the Old Testament has the admonition: 'Let us praise our famous men' (Ecclesiasticus, 44.1).

One may therefore say that, looked at historically, Shirley's sequence of Victor–Victim is reversed into Victim–Victor. In the final reckoning it is the Victor who gets the better of the Victim.

That also puts the individual neatly in his place. He is not rendered a superfluity in the universe on account of his mortality. He is a necessity like the leaves in a tree which maintain photosynthesis. The Cosmos is the everlasting deciduous tree which is kept alive by its leaves, growing anew and falling seasonally in turns. These seasons in the existence of man are in successive generations.

With this final conclusion I shall close my account of individualism.

Chapter 2

Of Nationalism

Following the method I adopted for discussing individualism, I shall first give the history and meanings of the words 'nation' and nationalism' as provided by the three dictionaries I am using, namely the *OED*, *Webster International,* and the *American Heritage Dictionary.*

The *OED*, of course, gives the history of the words, but as to their meanings it agrees with the others. Furthermore, there is in all three a clear definition of what the words 'nation' and 'nationalism' stand for, which was not to be found in respect of 'individualism'. All the dictionaries are precise in saying what 'nation' 'nationalism' are in themselves, which they were not in the case of 'individualism'.

The first thing to note is that the word 'nationalism' is not a primary word but a derivative of the word 'nation' through the derived adjective 'national'. What is not less striking is that the same long time interval separates the derivative from the original. The first citation of the word 'nation' in the *OED* is from AD 1300 whereas the derived abstract noun did not appear till 1836. The parallelism with Individualism is exact.

The *Webster International* gives six meanings of the word 'nationalism':
(1) National character, or tendency to it, nationality.
(2) An idiom, trait or character peculiar to any nation.
(3) Devotion to, or advocacy of national interests or national unity and independence.
(4) Zealous adherence to one's own nation or to its principles; patriotism.

(5) A phase of socialism.

(6) *Theological:* The doctrine that the people of a certain nation or nations are God's chosen people.

Of these, only the third and fourth meanings are relevant to the discussion in this chapter. But the full import and implications of these definitions cannot be realized without considering the meaning or meanings given by the dictionaries of the word 'nation'. This word, since it came into use in the middle ages has undergone a bewildering expansion and diversity of meanings. But for the present discussion only the modern meaning is relevant. Even this has many facets and nuances, and besides has thrown up such a penumbra round its highest centre that it is almost impossible to get a clear-cut view of nationalism. All the modern definitions of it agree broadly. Of these, it will be adequate to cite only the definition given in *Webster*. The dictionary could not make that short. Here it is:

> A people connected by supposed ties of blood generally manifested by community of language, religion, and customs and by a sense of common interest and interrelation.

> Popularly, any group of people having like institutions and customs and a sense of social homogeneity and mutual interest. Most nations are formed of agglomerations of tribes or peoples either of a common ethnic stock or of different stocks fused by long intercourse. A single language or closely related dialects, a common religion, a common tradition and history, a common sense of right and wrong, and a more or less compact territory, are typically characteristic, but one or more of these elements may be lacking and yet leave a group that from its community of interest and desire to lead a common life is called a *nation.*

As if this elasticity of the current definition of the word 'nation' was not a formidable difficulty in the way of a precise discussion of the subject, a greater difficulty has been created by the popular confusion between this word and certain other words. I am describing that in the words as given in *Webster's Dictionary of Synonyms*, which is very instructive. It is as follows:

Race, nation, people are frequently used as though they are interchangeable when they denote one of the great divisions of mankind, each of which is made up of an aggregate of persons who think of themselves or are thought of, as comprising a distinct unit. In present technical use, the terms are commonly differentiated in meaning.

Race is chiefly an anthropological and ethnological term; it usually implies a distinct physical type. One race is distinguished from another by its possession of certain unchanging characters, such as colour of the skin, the form of the hair, and the shape of the skull.

Nation is primarily a political term, but it is also common in historical writing and is even more frequent as a literary word with highly figurative connotations. It signifies the inhabitants, or more narrowly, the citizenry, of a sovereign state, or any body of persons who have been united under one independent government long enough to have acquired a distinct identity. But *nation* is often contrasted with *state*. J.R. Seeley wrote: 'When a state fell to pieces, the *nation* held together.' J.R. Green wrote: 'A state is accidental, it can be made or unmade, but a *nation* is something real which can be neither made nor destroyed.'

People is the preferred word in historical and sociological terminology, when a body of persons as a whole and as individuals show a consciousness of solidarity and of peculiarity that is not entirely explainable by *race* or *nation*. The term usually designates an aggregate of persons who, irrespective of their individual racial origins or ancestral nationalities, have through close and long-continued association achieved a common culture, common interests and ideals, and a sense of race or kinship.

This shows how difficult it would be for even a strict writer, not to speak of an average educated person, to keep the words apart and not to confuse them. But, however difficult, for a correct understanding of nationalism as it is today, the words must not be confused.

Nationalism and War

It is only from the end of the eighteenth century that wars have become connected with nationalism. Before that wars were waged by monarchs or states against other monarchs or states, and the masses of the people of the belligerent countries remained unconcerned. That is to say, wars were only policy pursued through military means, and never conflicts brought about by the collective hatred of one nation for another.

This transformation of the nature of wars was brought about by the American War of Independence (1775–83). It generated a lasting distrust and also hatred among Americans for Britain and the British people. This led to the war of 1812, which was called the 'Second War of American Independence', i.e. a war of national emancipation. The impact of this war on American nationalism was clearly described by an influential American politician, Albert Gallatin, who as Secretary of the Treasury was the adviser of two Presidents. After the end of the war in 1815, he wrote:

> The war has renewed and reinstated the national feelings and character which the Revolution had given, and which were daily lessening. The people have now more general objects of attachment, with which their pride and political opinions are connected. They are *more American* [italics mine], they feel and act more as a nation; and I hope that the permanency of the union is thereby better secured.

But the most thoroughgoing transformation of war from a monarchical, dynastic, state-conducted war to a national war, i.e. a war between peoples was brought about by the French Revolution from 1792 onwards.

In the summer of 1792, the Emigrés were waiting near the border of France to march to Paris and if possible release Louis XVI and the royal family. Behind were the Prussian and Austrian forces under the Duke of Brunswick. Their number was 84,000. To oppose them there were only 55,000 French troops of the disorganized regular army. In these circumstances, the French Assembly, on 11 July 1792, appealed to the French nation to join the army by declaring the Motherland to be in danger. It said:

> Numerous foreign troops are advancing towards our frontiers; all those who regard liberty in horror have armed themselves against our constitution. Citizens, the Motherland is in danger!

P. Sagnac, the author of the first volume of Lavisse's great history of contemporary France, comments on this:

> By this declaration, the Assembly laid on the people the task of saving themselves. Then the most insignificant workers, the poorest and the most illiterate of peasants learnt that their Motherland was in danger. That was after the 14th of July, 1789 (BastilleDay), the most important event of the Revolution. A nation was moved down to its deepest masses to resist the invaders.

It added half a million men to the French forces. These were indeed inexperienced and untrained. The French historian Lois Madelin wrote about them that they trembled before the invaders. But he added that they soon made Europe tremble before them.

This was the basic truth. As Albert Sord wrote in his monumental history of Europe and the French Revolution:

> The French Revolution, from its beginnings and by virtue of its first principles sapped the base and ruined the entire edifice of old monarchic Europe. It proclaimed the sovereignty of the people, presented its doctrines like self-evident and universal truths and threatened all established powers to revolt and emancipate themselves.

Before beginning his 'cannonade' at Valmy, Kellerman raised his hat on the tip of his sword and cried out 'Vive la nation!' His troops thundered back: 'Vive la nation!'

Old Europe failed to understand what was opposing it.

The infusion of nationalism into militarism and of militarism into nationalism took a further step in the Prussian War of Liberation against subjection to Napoleon after the battle of Jena. It was directed politically by Stein, militarily by Scharnhorst, who transformed the old mercenary army of Prussia into a national army.

The ideological campaign against French domination was carried on by Fichte and Jahn. Fichte made his contribution to the war of liberation by a series of lectures in which he put forward his idea of a true war, which drew a very subtle contrast between the positions of France and Germany in the war between the two.

F.L. Jahn was a pedagogue but also a patriot. He was the founder of the schools called Gymnasia, because these taught gymnastics. But their gymnastic exercises sought to revive the spirit of the German people by the development of their physical and moral powers. The young gymnasts were taught to regard themselves as members of a guild for the emancipation of their fatherland.

The war of liberation actually started in 1813 and culminated in the Battle of Leipzig in 16–19 October 1813. It was significantly called a 'Battle of Nations' and led finally to the abdication of Napoleon in 1814.

There were three wars of national liberation in the nineteenth century, namely the war in Germany and the Peninsula War in Spain; but the third for liberating northern Italy from Austrian domination was fought in 1859 and obtained its final victory on Solferino.

Nationalism and Imperialism

By the general acceptation of the meaning of the two words, these two political phenomena are supposed to be opposed, or even hostile to each other. It has been assumed that imperialism suppresses nationalism by imposing the domination of one powerful nation over others which are weaker than itself, and nationalism in its active form is a revolt against imperialism. The American revolution created this notion, and since then American political thinking has always been under its sway. This opposition was present in the mind of President F.D. Roosevelt, and in 1942, he compelled Britain to yield to it and send the Cripps Mission to India.

In reality, nationalism and imperialism are the same political urge, the first being its defensive aspect and the second its assertive.

Nationalism becomes imperialism when a nation becomes so powerful that it seeks to bring other nations under its domination, but it does not cease to practise nationalism for that reason; it simply asserts the power of nationalism at its highest and most expensive.

No great Indian thinkers of the nineteenth century, beginning with Ram Mohun Roy and ending with Bankim Chandra Chatterji regarded British rule in India as an evil thing. Although they regretted the subject status of themselves, they also asserted that British rule in India had in its effect been good for India. Imperialism has been so persistent all over the world through the ages that it is above slapdash judgements. Both ancient Iranians and Romans considered ruling over other nations as their moral obligation. My definition of imperialism follows:

There is no empire without a conglomeration of linguistically, racially, and agriculturally different nationalities and the hegemony of one of them over the rest. The heterogeneity and the domination are of the very essence of imperial relations. An empire is hierarchical. An empire is not inter-racially or internationally egalitarian.

I think I have been quite unambiguous in regard to the true character of imperialism.

Imperialism and Colonialism

Another mistake in contemporary political thinking is to confuse imperialism with colonialism. This mistake has led to calling the abandonment of their empires in Asia and Africa a process of 'decolonization'. No such political phenomenon as 'decolonization' has been seen in history. Colonization of any country by a foreign people has always become permanent. The United States was created by the colonization of people of British origins in North America. It has not been nor will ever be 'decolonized'.

Colonization is the settlement of foreign people in a country which had a truly national population, at times resulting in the total disappearance of the native population, at others in reducing it to a servile status.

Let me give some examples. The so-called Aryans or Indo-European-speaking people were foreign and certainly European colonists in India. Wherever they settled they reduced the original population to a servile and untouchable status. The 'pre-Aryan' natives of India were left free only in those areas in which the Aryans did not settle, mostly the hilly regions of southern and central India.

The Europeans were colonists in North America and South America, and brought about the same ethnic transformation. They were colonists in North Africa, East Africa and South Africa. They were also colonists in Australia and New Zealand.

But they were *not* colonists in West Africa, India, Burma, Malay, Indonesia and Indo-China. These were regions of European *imperialism*. This fundamental distinction between the two forms of European expansion in the world should never be overlooked.

The Present Position of Historic Nationalism

The account of nationalism just given is of its diverse aspects and expressions, as these were seen since this political sentiment made its first appearance in history. My object in doing this is to show how different nationalism has become in the contemporary world from what it was till now. What it is today cannot be related to what it was in history.

The two essential features of historic nationalism have wholly disappeared:

(1) It is no longer the desire or attempt to liberate a subject nation from foreign rule. With the exception of a small number of small nations which have voluntarily remained associated with their former rulers, all nations are now independent.

(2) Nationalism in its assertive and expansive form of imperialism has also disappeared. There is no country in the present-day world, however powerful it might be, which wants to bring another nation under its rule.

For me, this has been an unexpected development considering the future of Indian independence realized on 15 August 1947. In January 1948 I wrote in my *Autobiography of an Unknown Indian* (p. 507 of the English edition) that:

> I expect either the United States singly or a combination of the United States and the British Commonwealth [not *the* Commonwealth] to re-establish and rejuvenate the foreign domination of India.

No such possibility can be envisaged today. But I would still say that totally unforeseen circumstances can bring about a reversal of the present American outlook and policy.

I shall also add that in 1904 Anatole France wrote that he thought President Theodore Roosevelt was getting political inspiration from the Romans and going to make the United States an imperial power (see his book, *Sur la Pierre Blanche*).

Finally, I would say that the future is always unpredictable. So, in respect of imperialism, one may put up the hatchment *Requiescat in pace* or *Resurgan* according to one's wish.

Even so, one has to admit that nationalism in both its historical expressions is dead today. But we can still say: 'Nationalism is dead, long live Nationalism', for a new Nationalism like a new monarch has appeared. What is it like?

The New Nationalism

In trying to answer the question just raised I arrive at the main theme of this chapter: What is present-day nationalism? I shall give my conception of it systematically in the order of importance of its different features.

I. First and foremost, it is a self-sufficient and disinterested passion. National passion in the past always had two expressions: (1) pursuit of national interests or gains, for example territory, commercial opportunities and privileges, scope for colonial expansion; and (2) satisfaction of national pride or *amour-propre*. Among those people who are volubly nationalistic today, the pursuit of national interests has fallen into a second and minor place when it has not disappeared altogether. The main and the strongest drive for it comes from national pride.

II. The new nationalism has created a strong sense of national identity for each nation which is different from other national identities. Consciousness of being *we* not *they* is strong and ineradicable in the present-day nationalists. This makes them xenophobic. Of course, xenophobia is a very old feeling. All primitive peoples were not only hostile to strangers, but also killed and ate them. The

Greeks called all non-Greeks 'barbarians', the Indo-Aryans called all foreigners *mleccha,* which means the same thing as 'barbarian', or speakers of an unintelligible language. In all this, however, there was no hostility, only a sense of being different, with just a consciousness of superiority.

But in contemporary nationalism xenophobia has became aggressive and active. It has created a feeling that all foreigners are potential enemies.

III. The historic nationalism has virtually disappeared among the great nations of the world. When it is present among them it is just an acceptance of their identity without any aggressive or defensive application.

The new nationalism at its typical and strongest is found today only among those people who have been liberated from European imperialism. So it is *the* political passion of the 'freed-nations', which has created a type of human personality like the 'freed man' in Roman society, who although free could never forget that he had once been a slave.

This extensive transformation of the society of nationalistic peoples has given quite a new complexion to national pride. It has become largely a nationalistic inferiority complex. All the present-day nationalistic people of Asia and Africa have a feeling that they are confronted by hostile peoples, and nurse endless grievances.

IV. It is self-evident that a sense of grievance which cannot be got rid of generates hatred, and, as a rule, impotent hatred, which becomes unappeasable.

These are the four outstanding features of contemporary nationalism, and these are seen in four ethnic conflicts in the present-day world: (1) in India between the Hindus and the Muslims; (2) in the Middle East in the conflict between the Arabs and the Jews; (3) in the British Isles between the Roman Catholics of Ireland and the Protestants; and (4) between the Whites and the Blacks in South Africa.

The conflict in South Africa has for the present been brought to an end by the surrender of the Whites to the Blacks. Apparently, the Whites have become reconciled to being dominated by the

Blacks. But whether this submission will last or how long it will, no one can say. It is one of the indisputable facts of history that friendship between nations is fragile, while hatred is ineradicable. In respect of strength, love can never be equal to hatred.

Therefore, nationalism among the peoples of Asia and Africa has led to repeated and continuing armed conflicts. Yet they have been indecisive.

The active and practical expression of nationalism among the peoples of Asia and Africa is seen in two forms: first, in excessive military preparation and unbearable burden of military expenditure; secondly, in terrorism. As things appear today, both seem to be irremovable.

There is not the slightest hope that any real gain or profit will come to any side from these two. Yet both are continuing. There is only word-mongering against them.

Military burden and expenditure in these countries have become only a competitive deterrent, a means of intimidating the rival. Competition for nuclear arms has entered into this military effort.

Terrorism, on the other hand, has not got even this exiguous practical justification. It is just satisfaction of hatred, pure hatred prized for the enjoyment it gives to those who fall into its clutches.

In giving this account (and by implication an assessment) of the latest form of nationalism, I have only put it in its proper place in the mental life of the mankind of our times. This life has one overriding emotion: hatred generated by conflicts of every kind, personal and social. Everybody in it is at odds with everybody else, and therefore every nation can be expected to be against every other. The Old Order changeth yielding place to New, lest one good custom should spoil the world.

Chapter 3

Of Democracy

In this part of my book I am describing individualism, nationalism and democracy as agents of the decline and fall of Western civilization in their present form. Therefore, my consideration of democracy will not be its political exercise, but its extension to all aspects of contemporary life, economic, social and cultural. Democracy, which literally means rule or domination of the Demos, the people, is now a passion working on the entire life of a nation, and it makes that life conform to the opinions, wishes, and preferences of the largest number of persons constituting it. It is, in a word, the domination (for some the tyranny) of the majority.

This comprehensive form of democracy is a very recent creation, as time is reckoned in history. In order to realize its significance it is necessary to give a brief resumé of democracy as it has been seen over about two thousand five hundred years of its existence.

It was recognized and described as a form of government by Athenian philosophers, more specifically by Plato and Aristotle. Before this, government everywhere was monarchic and accepted as the rule of a person or a dynasty. Different forms of government appeared after the abolition of monarchy and also abrogation or limitation of monarchies in certain countries or cities.

It was Plato who first discussed the character of democracy, and he was hostile to it. His judgement was that adoption of democracy would be to hand over the government of the city (*Pols*, which really meant the city as an independent state) to the least educated, least cultured, least steady and most whimsical element in its population.

But it has to be pointed out that in Athens (and by imitation in other Greek cities) democracy did not mean government by the entire body of its inhabitants. It was a right of the 'citizens' only, and the working population was almost wholly slaves, who could not be citizens. In Athens, being aristocratic or democratic simply stood for belonging or not belonging to the old families distinguished by birth and social superiority established by prescription.

The Greek notion and practice of democracy did not create the modern democracies in the West. Therefore, it may be disregarded in the discussion of democracy for my purpose in this book.

Modern Democracy

'Modern democracy' is really the American democracy as created by the breaking away of the thirteen American colonies from the British connection. Its fundamental principle was enunciated in the opening passage of the Declaration of Independence adopted on 4 July 1776. The relevant passage is as follows:

> All men are created equal, they are endowed by their Creator with certain unalienable Rights, among these are Life, Liberty and the pursuit of happiness; to ensure these rights, Governments are instituted among Men, deriving their just powers from the consent of the governed; whenever any Form of Government become destructive of these ends, it is the Right of the People to alter or abolish it, and to institute new Governments most likely to effect this Safety and Happiness.

The fundamental doctrine of American democracy that it was the 'government of the people, by the people, and for the people' was asserted by Lincoln in his famous address to commemorate the dead in the Battle of Gettysburg, delivered on 19 November 1863. It was fought to ensure whether the proposition laid down by the Founding Fathers that 'all men are created equal' could endure.

Lincoln had previously expressed his confidence in the judgement of a people taken as a whole in these famous words: 'You can fool all the people some of the time, and some people all the time, but you cannot fool all the people all of the time.' It was simply the reiteration of the old saying: *Vox populi, Vox Dei* (the voice of the people is the voice of the God) and of the Islamic dogma that the *ijma* (collective opinion) of a whole people cannot be wrong. Lincoln could not foresee the power of television to fool all the people all the time.

The two classical descriptions of democracy as it was in America were given by Alexis de Tocqueville in his *Democracy in America* and by James (Sond) Bryce in two books *The American Common-wealth* (1888) and *Modern Democracies* (1921). These books formed the idea of democracy in persons of my generation. As a result, political democracy came to be accepted as the best and most just form of government by all who were not narrowly conservative or influenced by the new distrust of democracy among French intellectuals.

This belief in democracy was further strengthened by World War I both in America and Britain. The Allied Powers were assumed to be champions of freedom as against authoritarianism. In England, the sociologist Thomas Hobhouse popularized the idea and President Wilson gave it great authority by asserting it in his Fourteen Points. He explained that among the ends sought to be achieved by his Fourteen Points was this: 'The settlement of every question of territory, of sovereignty, of economic arrangement, or of political relationship must be upon the basis of the free acceptance of that settlement by the people immediately concerned, and not upon the basis of material interest or advantage of another nation.'

Democracy in the Inter-War Years (1922–39)

Democracy after World War I did not, however, run along the lines which the Versailles settlement envisaged. Instead, being a coherent democracy in the form representative of parliamentary government, it showed another form in the emergence of plebiscitary dictatorship in Italy and Germany. Although these were popularly supposed to be opposed and antagonistic, at bottom they were one, both based on the wish of the majority of the people concerned. In actual fact, the will of the majority of people in both Italy and Germany was more united and assertive in these two than in the countries with parliamentary governments.

The Soviet dictatorship was not indeed accepted by the general mass of the people of the Union, but the Soviet dictator preserved the form of election. Only, its result was always a foregone conclusion.

Anyway, these two forms of democracy clashed in 1939 and were at war from 1939 to 1945. The defeat of Germany and Italy, brought about paradoxically with the co-operation of the Soviet dictatorship, finally made parliamentary and representative government the universal and only form of democracy. This is the democratic 'establishment' all over the world today as far as politics is concerned. It is practised as normal, raising no discussion of its merits or demerits. It is both dull and uninspiring.

The Advent of Total Democracy

The democratic ideology or dogma which is not only assertive but aggressive today, may be called 'total democracy' like 'total war'. It seeks to assert democratic power over all aspects of life, including the economic, social, cultural and educational. All these aspects of life must be given the form desired by the largest mass of the people. The opponents of this self-assertion of total democracy are stigmatized as 'élitist'.

The dictionary definition of an élite is that part of any society which is admitted to be and accepted as socially and mentally superior, and therefore entitled to regulate all activities and aims of that society. Élite is a term which recognizes 'quality' as the supreme criterion of determining the importance of any group of persons in the nation or community.

This standard is rejected by 'total democracy', which preaches and has popularized the notion that an élite is really an ideological *canaille*, a residual scum. The fanaticism shown by the holders of this view of 'élitism' is terrifying to those who prize quality. The 'total democracy' of today is, in contrast, the champion of quantity.

Egalitarianism has thus become the same as democracy everywhere, and most conspicuously among the English people.

Contemporary Egalitarianism

This social extension of democracy through the doctrine of equality has created as its corollary a new social function for governments. It is the creation of a classless society. Even the Conservative government of Britain has adopted and proclaimed that as its policy. This, however, is a reversal of the relationship between a society and a government. This results in a government which is expected to create a society, instead of a society a government, and that society is to be that which their egalitarian electorate wants. The government must adopt an egalitarian policy in order to remain in office. The electorate has succeeded in imposing its will on the government.

In order to realize the significance of this form of egalitarianism, it is necessary to review the history of the political and social dogma of equality since it was first propounded by the creators of the United States. They had made it absolute. In the next historical step, taken by the leaders of the French Revolution, the doctrine of equality was modified, radically.

In the Declaration of the Rights of Man adopted by the French National Assembly in August 1789 (which incidentally was approved by the King, Louis XVI), it was set down:

> Les hommes naissent et demeurent Libres et égaux en droits; les distinctions sociales ne peuvent être fondées que sur l'utilité' commune

> [Men are born and remain free by virtue of laws; social distinctions can be based only on common utility].

It is not necessary to point out how this declaration of equality differs from the American; furthermore, even social distinctions are admitted to have their utility in the egalitarian new order.

Even this conception of equality and all the subsequent development of the conception has been left behind by the contemporary advocates of equality. Their idea is that men are equal comprehensively and there can be no superiority or inferiority of any kind among them.

But there is a glaring inconsistency in the contemporary form of egalitarianism which reveals its true character. The egalitarians of today do not say that there is no inequality in the physical powers and skills of men. Not even the most fanatical egalitarian of today claims that the boxer, football player, runner, jumper, weight lifter is equal to other exhibitors of these feats of physical prowess. They do not say that any pop singer is equal to any other. They do not even say that one buffoon is exactly like all other buffoons. The inequalities are accepted as natural by the contemporary champions of equality.

The real egalitarianism of today is in respect of mental powers. The contemporary egalitarians assert, and assert with fierce fanaticism, that all men are equal in mental capacity. They assault anyone who would say that there is difference of intelligence among men. The attack of contemporary egalitarianism is on the human mind. It must be reduced to its lowest common denominator.

What drives this hostility to the human mind is easy to discover. The creative function of man is exercised by the mind and all creation is creation of inequality. The sharing of the gains through creation is brought about by a subsequent application of the sense of justice, which is aimed at making all men receiving these gains possess them to the extent of their capacity to create them. But, for contemporary egalitarians, there is no question of sharing something which does not exist. The acceptance of the idea of sharing appears to them as the prospect of becoming beggars, at best in an almshouse.

From this point in the inquiry into the character of contemporary egalitarianism it is easy to arrive at a valid, if not wholly correct, diagnosis of it. Not to put too fine a point on it: it is the assertion of the rancour of the futureless.

About six decades ago, a distinguished Frenchman of letters wrote a book entitled *Caliban Parle* ('Caliban Speaks'). He said that Caliban was expressing his resentment at being deprived of his rightful inheritance from his mother Sycorax and was trying to recover it from Prospero.

Caliban in his subjection to Prospero said:

> This island's mine, by Sycorax, my mother;
> Which thou tak'st from me.
> When thou camest first
> Thou mad'st much of me,
> Then I lov'd thee
> And show'd thee all the qualities o' th' isle...
> Cursed be I that did so!
> But
> You taught me language; and my profit on't
> Is, I know how to curse: the red plague rid
> You,
> For learning me your language.

With the coming of shipwrecked men he made common cause with them and thought he would recover his inheritance.

He already thought that he had got back his freedom and cried:

> High-day! high-day; freedom!
> Freedom! high-day freedom.

Since then Caliban has ceased to be militant—he is triumphant.

Herein lies the victory of the egalitarian and his aim to convert democracy into equality.

This transformation of democracy makes it one of the three agents of the decline and fall of Western civilization.

I shall now pass on to a consideration of the decline and fall, so far as it has progressed, in Britain, India and the United States.

PART THREE

Decline and Fall of Western Civilization with its Worldwide Offshoots

Then, with no throbs of fiery pain
  No cold gradations of decay,
Death broke at once the vital chain...

  —Samuel Johnson

My perception of it—

Musing on the ruins behind St Paul's in London in April 1955, while a chanted service was going on inside it, I felt the apprehension of a possible decline and fall of Western civilization.

Chapter 1

Decadence of Western Civilization

In this part of the book I am going to describe the onset of the process of the 'decline and fall' of Western civilization, not its completion. This preliminary phase I am calling 'Decadence'. I shall presently clarify what I mean when I employ that word; here I would only say that a somewhat lengthy clarification will be needed, for no word has been, or is being, more misused.

In the meanwhile, I shall only assert that the decline and fall of civilizations is a real historical phenomenon, which has again and again been seen in history. There is no doubt that civilizations of ancient Egypt, Mesopotamia (historically known as Assyrio-Babylonian), Iran, Greece and Rome disappeared. So did, to my thinking, the Chinese, which was one of the original human civilizations. That the ancient Indian also did is *my* view, but not accepted by present-day Hindus. I shall give the reasons for my view in their proper place. Here I am only setting down the bare enunciation.

I hope I have now made the scope of this part of the book unambiguous. But what still remains unexplained is my understanding and concept of decadence. I shall now set that down precisely. I was first alerted about employing the word by two critics: Remy de Gourmont of France and Middleton Murry in England. Since then I have never succumbed to vague impressions in using it, in all its denotations and connotations.

I shall begin my classification by listing the meanings given to it by the two dictionaries I am using: *Webster International* and *OED*.

The *Webster International* gives a number of meanings, but its ancillary dictionary—that of synonyms—gives what I regard as the most accurate definition. Bringing the word into relationship with 'deterioration', 'degeneration', 'devolution', 'decline' and 'declension', the dictionary gives the particular meaning of the word:

> Decadence 'presupposes a previous maturing and usually a high degree of excellence; it implies that the falling takes place after a thing (such as a people, a literature or other form of art, a branch of knowledge) has reached the peak of its development.

The *OED* sets forth its various meanings, and its first citation is from the sixteenth century. Its definitions range from social and cultural phenomena to the physical, e.g. 'decadence of man', for falling of hair with age.

It is unnecessary to take note of all those meanings; one may accept 'decadence' as the correct word for the definition given in the *Webster's Dictionary of Synonyms*.

But the word has also acquired a number of moral associations, almost wholly pejorative, bringing suggestions of corruption and degeneracy with it. In my consideration of decadence, I shall strictly divest the word of its moral connotations. Thus I would say that a nation in decadence is like an ageing man who has lost his physical vigour, shows signs of bodily decrepitude, has lost his mental powers, especially the creative, and has sunk into a narrow conservatism. Wordsworth certainly showed the course of this shrinkage from youth to age. But no man should be blamed for submitting to a natural process.

Applied to a nation, I would say that it is decadent when it has lost its political and economic power as well as its cultural creativeness. I must further make it clear that continuing changes in a society must not be taken in their totality as creative activity. They might not have any cultural significance and might even be steps towards decline.

I shall give two instances of collective or national decadence from history. The first is of the late Hellenistic stage of Greek civilization; and the second, the last stage of the Roman Empire after the reign of Diocletian (AD 284–313). I might add flippantly that I consider Mrs Thatcher (deified post-premierly as the Baroness Thatcher) as the British Diocletian in a female incarnation.

National decadence is existing only in a state of being to which the future sends no call and offers no promise, and which therefore is an escapist's life of delusions.

Last of all, in considering the emergence of decadence in our age, I have to point out that 'decadence' as decline from a higher state to a lower one (including even physical stature in human beings) was considered to be the natural order of evolution of human life by all peoples and in all countries since the beginning of recorded history. Man's 'golden age' was always relegated to the past. Horace proclaimed the view in the most famous words about decadence:

Aetas parentum peior avis tulit
　　Nos nesquiores, mox daturos
Progeniem Vitiosiorum.

[Our Fathers' age was worse than our grandfathers'. We their more worthless sons will procreate in our turn a progeny more corrupt.]

This view of a qualitative procession of human generation dominated opinion for ages and was challenged and rejected only in the nineteenth century. I first read about this revolution of opinion in 1922 in the famous Romance Lecture which Dean Inge delivered in 1920.

It made a deep impression on me, and made me aware of a conflict, oscillating in its operation from one extreme to another, between progress and decadence. I had already been brought to a pessimistic mood regarding the opposition between good and evil, the progressive trend and the declining, by my reading of our great epics. Both of them told the story of a great victory followed by a disconcerting defeat.

This was reinforced in me by my reading of Greek history. I was shocked by the defeat of Athens at the hands of Sparta in the Peloponnesian War. I seemed to hear the clang of the pickaxes which were demolishing the walls from Athens to Peiraeus. I thought, if that was to be the end for Athens, why was the Persian war fought at all. All human achievements began to stand before my eyes with unpredictable and undeserved doom hanging over them.

But I could not foresee that I would have to contemplate the future of civilization in my old age with an inescapable despair. I have to describe what I am forced to witness.

Chapter 2

Decadence of the English People

Part I: The Decadence

How Fear Came

For all who prize life or existence, fear is like the fuse in an electric circuit; it protects or at least alerts people that protection is needed. It is not cowardly.

Strangely enough, fear about the future of the English people insinuated itself in my mind at the very time when I got a first-hand impression of the greatness of English life and civilization: in 1955 when for the first time I came to England at the age of fifty-seven.

Many Englishmen asked me then whether I was disappointed by what I was finding and seeing. They explained their question by adding that all Indians came to England with a very romantic idea of the country and got a shock from their actual meeting with it. I at once answered that there was no disappointment in me; on the contrary, my actual experience was confirming my conceptions, however romantic they might have been. For me, it was like Sleeping Beauty waking up.

As a result of this experience, my stay of only five weeks produced my book on England, which was published in 1959 and had 229 pages. It flowed with an unqualified expression of happiness in its first three parts: the English scene, the English people, cultural life. Only the last part, called 'State of the Nation', gave expression to misgivings in questions like 'The Welfare State, Fact or Hoax' and an explicit conviction like 'Farewell to Politics'. This part ended with a chapter entitled 'National Destiny'.

In it I put to myself the most fundamental question which arose in my mind: Were they going to recover their old position or create a new position of which they could be as proud, or were they to slide down the path of inevitable decline? I am quoting these words from the book which was published in 1959.

During my stay in England, I put the question to an English friend whether there was any thinking on the national destiny among his people. He promptly replied that there was none.

The question would not leave my mind. Thus, when I was in Rome in the last stage of my sojourn abroad, I expressed my misgivings to my hostess, who was the daughter of Robert Graves. She replied:

> You see, Mr Chaudhuri, we have had very bad times and we have come through, although we hardly knew how to. We have also recovered more rapidly than we could have believed to be possible. I think that is why we are enjoying the present for a little while. I am sure we are not really thoughtless about the future.

After that I felt reassured for the time being, but the question never left my mind, and in the coming years it became more and more insistent, and at last even forced me to a provisional answer that decline was in the offing.

I need not describe the stages in which my fears were confirmed by my subsequent visits to England in 1967 and 1968, until in 1970, when I came to England never to return to my country and to settle there, my premonitions of decadence in England finally became a conviction gaining with the years an accelerated force.

As I am writing these lines I am being ridden by it as Sindbad was by the Old Man of the Sea, but I am incapable of shaking it off.

The All-embracing Faces of English Decadence

There is not a single aspect of English life to which decadence is not spreading and deepening its invasion—national personality, politics, social and economic life, education and culture.

Just to give an indication of this invasion of total envelopment, I shall choose one or two instances. These may seem trivial, but their triviality is only in their place in national life, not in their significance for it.

The first indication is being given by the revolution in the attitude to expense. The attitude to expenditure of money is a very important clue to character and personality. I think Molière's *Avare* (Miser) to be more dangerous than his *Tartuffe* (Hypocrite). In fact, by showing how a man could become inhuman on account of his love of money Molière himself reveals that he thought so too.

I now give the example to which this rather pompous introduction leads. During my stay in England in 1955, I spoke to a lady about shops in a certain street in London. Her reply was: 'Frightfully cheap!' Nowadays, when people see an article of clothing on me which they think is very stylish they ask me where I got it. When I name my tailors, they remark, 'Are they not expensive?' Shopping around has became a habit, and one which repels me.

My next example is a more serious one: the Princess Diana affair with its pendants. My wife and I were unable to share the enthusiasm which her marriage evoked. Somehow, her looks (in spite of our partial admission of her beauty) and her behaviour gave us a feeling that she was not of the class to which a Princess of Wales should belong. We were never able to get rid of this impression of incompatibility. Now, I would say that our impression, vague as it was, has been justified.

But the affair has not become what it now appears to be on account of any personal failing in the Princess, exclusive to herself. It seems to be part of a decline in the character of the Spencer family of Althorp. I had acquired a very great respect for the family and the house from my reading of English history in my student days. Both seemed now to have slipped down to a lower level.

Certainly, Princess Diana has neither the looks nor the air of Georgiana, Countess of Spencer, nor of her young daughter, as represented in the painting by Reynolds, which is at Althorp.

More especially, life at Althorp is not what it was at the end of the last century. I give a description of it, which I read in Lord Morley's *Recollections*:

> After dinner we went into what I do think was the most fascinating room I ever saw in a house—great or small—one of the libraries, lined with well-bound books on white enamelled shelves, with a few, but not too many knick-knacks lying about, and all illuminated with the soft radiance of many clusters of wax candles. A picture to remember: Spencer with his noble carriage and fine red beard; Mr G [Gladstone] seated on a low stool, discoursing as usual, playful, keen, versatile; Rosebery saying little, but now and then launching a pleasant *mot;* Harcourt cheery, expansive, witty.

This description is followed by another, which was of a meeting the next morning:

> We met in the famous room where all the sovereign treasures of the bibliomaniacs are—the Caxtons, the Mazarin Bible, the Mainz Psalter; ...Rosebery took up a book and turned it sedulously over, only interjecting a dry word now and then. Harcourt not diffuse...

Spencer went to Morley's room:

> Spencer came into my room betimes in his pink, to return letters and say good-bye. He was off for a fourteen-mile drive to the meet, and the rain pouring.

Now to take note of life at Althorp today. I read the following news in the Business Supplement of *Sunday Telegraph* of 19 November 1995:

> Earl Spencer, the Princess of Wales' brother, has opened the door of their family seat, Althorp House in Northamptonshire, to big business in an effort to fund its heavy running costs. The stately house is for hire for meetings or corporate entertainment for as little as £3,500 a day.
>
> The earl has hired the former hotelier David Horton-Fawkes to run the house as a commercial enterprise. The state dining room seats up to 150, while meetings can be held in the stunning picture gallery which contains several Van Dyck masterpieces.
>
> The earl has taken this step because the upkeep of Althorp costs £400,000 a year.

The philosophy of Althorp is to serve the client first and to be a stately home second, he said.

I do not think that even the contrast between the old description and the present transformation of Althorp will be perceived today, not to speak of shocking anybody. The employment of the word 'philosophy' to characterize the transformation is trebly significant. What I have said till now I shall describe as my 'Impression' of English decadence in the maxim of Monet's picture 'Impression', which has been described as a 'neural and immediate psychical effect of sensory stimulus'.

I must now extend it to a more detailed and literal account of English decadence.

Part II: Aspects of the Decadence

General

Considered in its widest manifestation, the decadence is revealing itself in two forms: the general, which is like an incurable chronic disease, showing no obvious dangerous symptoms, nevertheless debilitating in its effects, and in the final result fatal, but not sensationally. So the danger is insidious.

The second manifestation is malignant, violent and alarming, like the sudden outbreak of a plague, smallpox or cholera epidemic. It is like these diseases before the modern methods of checking them were discovered. So it frightens and almost paralyses the mind when it is met with.

I shall describe the general incidence of decadence first, in its various manifestations; and indeed they are many.

Falsity of Behaviour

This is starkly seen in the fact that living among the English people today is no longer living naturally, that is to say, being sincere and un-selfconscious in conduct. It has become posing, men and women appearing as actors and actresses. They pose, not merely for the

79

sake of posturing, but to be photographed in their postures so that a wide public may see their poses and be impressed by these.

Providers of all kinds of goods are also more concerned with the package and name of the goods than their substance. This extends to authors also. When anyone learns that I am writing a book, the immediate query is: 'What have you called it', not what it is about. A wine shop, when I first entered it was known as Peter Dominque's, now it has taken the picturesque name of 'Bottoms up'.

Above all, if a person receives an honour he or she stands displaying the insignia of the honour with an elated expression, whose visible form might be anything from a simper to a grin.

On other occasions, these postures indicate that something has happened to the persons to make them angry, startled, afraid or pleased. Among young women, the posturing is most widely seen in the cult that becoming models has become. The desire to become a model has become so strong among these young persons that it may be regarded as their supreme ambition. The self-conscious artificiality of their postures is spectacular. The same spectacularity is seen in their facial expressions. No one can explain why they appear to be in a fit of rage, abandonment to sorrow, softened by tenderness, or brightened by amusement. The expressions are seen, but their causes are absent.

The impingement of this posturing on its objects has to be taken seriously. It is brought about in two ways: as 'stills' in the statues placed in shop-windows, and as 'movies' through TV and video. Thus even their living exhibition is becoming its vicarious impact and the transformation of experience of life into vicarious experience is one of the most noticeable features of contemporary decadence.

Falsity and Incongruity in Adornment

Englishwomen, especially the young, seem these days to have fallen for the Oriental habit of overloading themselves with jewellery in their workaday appearance. They appear with strings of pearls as big as sparrow's eggs round their necks, and heavy gold bangles round their wrists. But on them these are unoriental, for the pearls are synthetic and the gold fake. To speak of the gold only, a respectable Oriental woman would have only 22 carat.

In their 'above-the-belt' appearance these women seem to imitate the Hindu bayadère without really knowing what a bayadère was. They could have got a correct idea of her appearance from a ballet of Petipa, which was recently shown on BBC.

But the difference goes further. No bayadère, for that matter even an Oriental woman of today, would wear jewellery with jeans as the lower garment. That would make the upper and lower parts of the body not only incongruous, but repulsive. I perceive that whenever I have to stand in a queue in a superstore. The spectacle that I am compelled to see does not remind me even of the radical contrast that is seen between the upper and lower marine part of the body of a mermaid of fables. Instead of being unattractive the mermaid's lower part had a continuity of line and plasticity which is alluring.

Another kind of falsification among present-day Englishwomen is seen in their treatment of hair. Not only is natural hair differently coloured and dressed from day to day according to the whims of the women, wigs of a variety of form and colour are kept and used by them, particularly by the elderly. Thus falsification of adornment has become a feature of contemporary decadence.

Impact of Decadence on the English Character

Some time ago, *The Times* tried to find out through an opinion poll, which English poem was the favourite of the English people today. It was Kipling's *If-*, included in one of the stories in the collection *Rewards and Fairies* published in 1910 (reprinted in *Rudyard Kipling's Verse*: definitive edition, pp. 576 f). It laid down eighteen contingencies and suggested what were the right responses to them, and if the responses were such, it declared:

> Yours is the Earth and everything that's in it
> And—which is more—you'll be a Man, my son!

To give an idea of the contingencies envisaged I shall cite *only one.*

If you can force your heart and nerve and sinew
To serve your turn long after they are gone,
And so hold on when there is nothing in you
Except the Will which always says to them
'Hold on!'

Certainly, those who voted for the poem thought that the time had arrived to take stock of their power to meet these contingencies. But there must also have been a feeling that not only the eleventh, but even the twelfth hour had struck. The English people have become almost incapable of meeting the contingencies with the right responses. The choice of the poem by them must have been the last cry short of the cry of total despair.

Indeed, the hour for the last stand for the English character had come. I would amplify that observation by recalling what was the opinion of Indian nationalists about it. Even the most extreme among them did not dispute the following:

(1) That the English people were the most honest in the world.

(2) That the English people were the most disciplined in the world.

(3) That the English people were the most industrious in the world.

(4) That the English people could always be trusted to keep their word.

I shall not set down what, to my thinking, has happened to these virtues. Every Englishman I have met during my unbroken sojoun of nearly twenty-six years in England has admitted what could not be denied.

I shall give only one example of the present conditions. English families when they went abroad on a holiday always left the key of the house under the mat before the front door for the woman caretaker to come and clean the house. I saw that even in 1955, when I came to England for the first time.

Now I cannot leave my front door unlocked even when I am in the living room, very near the door, and my neighbour who lives in the maisonette above mine, never opens his front door without looking through the chained panels to see who has come and that too with a loaded baton in his hand. When I mention this condition to anybody I get the stereotyped answer of submission to circumstances: 'Things have changed!' This is acquiescence to a steady lowering of the standard of living.

Two Passions Typical of Decadence

These are first, the dominant, and secondly, the complementary and compensatory. Just to name them, the first is love of money in the extreme form of addiction, and unceasing pursuit of it; the second is licentiousness, indulgence in which is brought about by the necessity to counteract the insensitiveness generated by the pursuit of money. In decadence, the two, which would seem to have no connection with each other, become inseparably associated.

Among a decadent people money becomes an end in itself, instead of being the means to an end. In the nineteenth century the great American plutocrats were like the old conquistadors, in economic incarnation. The modern seekers of money at their most innocent are merely like ants or working bees. There is zoological innocence in their activity; but in man's pursuit of money it acquires moral repulsiveness by becoming wholly sordid.

The sordidness becomes immoral when money-making becomes unscrupulous, and almost all money-making today is such. The absence of scruples illustrates the dictum that those who think money can do everything are also those who are ready to do everything for money.

The contemporary love of money is also seen in an active form as ostentation by a section of the new rich. In them, the employment of money has become what it never was in the English aristocracy. Among them, it was taken as a matter of course, nothing to be conscious of by themselves or noticeable by others. That unconsciousness has been wholly lost. The assertive minority of the wealthy today display their wealth with vulgar garishness. When in possession of money they are like inflated balloons; but since they also squander it recklessly, they soon become deflated balloons.

Turning now to the compensatory passion of contemporary devotion towards licentiousness, I have to say that the character it shows is totally different from every kind of licentiousness I have read about. In a Johnsonian phrase I can say, 'I have surveyed licentiousness from China to Peru.' I have read descriptions of it as it was in Japan, China, India, the Islamic world, and in Europe, more especially in Europe in all the majors works from De Brantome to Casanova. I have also seen depictions of it in painting and sculpture by Etruscans, Romans, Greeks, Indians, Chinese, and above all the Japanese. The Japanese Shunga is the most artistic and at the same time most exciting of all erotic paintings.

But even so, I could not imagine that licentiousness could assume so crude, coarse and mindless a form as it has assumed now. I shall speak of its malignant form later. In its normal form it is as insipid as dust and yet repulsive. It has become mere indulgence in tactile sensation, which nevertheless is amplified by an injection of dirtiness. Activities like eating and sexual congress when barely seen are neutral in their exhibition. But in its contemporary indulgence sexual intercourse has acquired some piquancy. But piquancy is too literary a word to apply to it. It is—in plain language—itch.

Decadence and Government

The appearance of decadence in government is today seen concretely; it is not simply subjectively detected. In all countries, in past times, decadence of government was seen in three features: bureaucracy, high taxation and debasement of money. One of its notable appearances was between the reign of Septimius Severus up to the reign of Diocletian in the Roman Empire, i.e. from about AD 225 to 275. Money meant nothing then except in large amounts, and coinage was debased. Diocletian checked it for the time being. But the decadent features reappeared. In the Byzantine empire it was seen conspicuously in the power of the bureaucracy.

In modern times, the grip of a bureaucracy on governing was seen at its strongest in czarist Russia in the last decades of czardom. It stifled all effectual political activity. But I now perceive that a bureaucracy, called the Civil Service, was acquiring the same hold on government in Britain when I first came to that country in 1955.

This feeling I embodied in two chapters of my book *A Passage to England,* which was published in 1959, and these chapters are entitled 'A Constitution Parliament' and 'Farewell to Politics'. (pp. 185–98).

I shall give an idea of the revelation I got. I said in the book that to all politically minded Indians the House of Commons was like the political Mecca with its stone of Kaaba. But when I actually saw a session of it the mental impression created within me affected me very peculiarly, I could not bring myself to believe that what I was seeing and hearing was in any way connected with government, that is with the cruel trade of politics in which good nature had no place.

I got the impression that everybody in that chamber was conforming to a pre-established pattern of behaviour, which laid down that the debates should have an air of high-spirited and even angry contests, and yet mean nothing at all.

In respect of political life, I was forced to the conclusion that the English people had lost not only their political ambition but also the greater part of their zest in politics.

However, I saw nothing to blame in this. It seemed to be a natural evolution. But what I resented was the power of catchwords. Their flow was in inverse proportion to their truth.

The conversion of the House of Commons to a mere stage for acting before the electorate has pursued its relentless course since then. It has been completed by the introduction of TV into the House of Commons. The MPs no longer discuss public affairs in it, they only declaim and posture before the people. This is real decadence of parliamentary government.

Political Leadership in Decadence

Yet, formally, the head of this parliamentary and representative government seems to have acquired a status which suggests power. In respect of Mrs Thatcher, the newspapers wrote that Thatcher orders this or orders that; the papers are writing in the same way about Mr Major. Never before was the decision of the English government described as the order of a Prime Minister. During the war when Churchill was virtually a dictator, his decisions had to be confirmed by a council and was regarded as a collective decision. At times he was overruled by his colleagues and had to abide by their decision.

What, then, has happened since those times that a British Prime Minister can now send an order like a dictator, as if he occupied a position like Mussolini, Hitler, or Stalin. This certainly appears to confirm the opinion of Plato that democracy leads to tyranny in the Greek sense.

Yet, these orders do not make any difference to the course of events. The British people have not got a real plebiscitary dictator, although the newspapers write as if there is one. Thus Mrs Thatcher was regarded as such, and even Mr Major is, although he certainly does not exercise the same power.

Impact of Decadence on Religion and Morality
The impact of decadence on religion and morality among the English people today has brought about, in respect of religion, a total reversal of the relationship between a people and their religion. Not to speak of civilized people in historic times, even among primitive people in prehistoric times, it was their religion which controlled their life. To give an example of this from history, in India among the Hindus, even down to recent times, religious inhibitions and taboos regulated even food habits and attire. To disregard even the most trivial of these was to lose caste, to be driven outside the pale and made untouchable.

But what I am seeing today in Britain is the opposite: control and reshaping of religion by the people in accordance with their wishes and whims. The religion of the English people must now be what they wish it to be.

This reversal has been accepted by the highest *ex officio* authority over the practice of Christianity by the English people—the Anglican Church. Its prelates by a majority have decided to obey the voice of the people as the voice of God. They have, in the truest sense of the words, become demagogues as a class.

They do not admit that by so doing they are rejecting their traditional Christianity. They say:

Think not that I am come to destroy the law, or the prophets; I am not come to destroy but to fulfil.

This is the strangest part of their somersault in respect of their religion: this reiteration of the declaration put in the mouth of Jesus (Matthew, v. 17).

Therefore, there is, so to speak, an imaginary dialogue between me and the dignitaries of the Anglican Establishment:

'You are old, Father William,' the young man said,
'And your hair has become very white;
And yet you incessantly stand on your head—
Do you think, at your age, it is right.'
'In my youth,' Father William replied to his son,
'I feared it might injure the brain;
But, now that I'm perfectly sure I have none,
Why, I do it again and again.'

I am afraid of continuing the argument, for I am convinced that Father William will say: 'Be off, or I'll kick you downstairs.'

Even Royal supremacy over the Anglican Church, which was set down as absolute except in matters of doctrine, in the Thirty-seventh Article of the Thirty-nine Articles, the Charter under which the Anglican Church after the Reformation has operated, is now being challenged.

Last of all, I have to say that although faith in Christianity has virtually disappeared among the English, except where it is a lifeless regional loyalty in elderly people, superstition has become more powerful than ever. This has been seen as a natural sequence in the evolution of all religions. Whenever a religion has ceased to be living its heir has been superstition, which is of course older than religion and was its precursor.

I have next to consider the impact of decadence on morality. Among them morality was always closely associated with Christianity. Therefore, with the decline and even disappearance of faith in Christianity, it has been easy for the English people to shed all their moral inhibitions and liberate themselves from morality. This is a drastic and comprehensive revolution. Although most blatantly

87

seen in respect of sexual life, it also covers all moral inhibitions, for example in regard to stealing and even homicide.

It is unnecessary for me to give examples of the rejection of morality in all human activities in Britain. Anyone reading the newspaper in the morning will get enough for one day. Indeed, I might say that in respect of this, Decadance crieth without; She uttereth her voice in the streets; She crieth in the chief places of concourse.

So I shall only set down what the New Testament pronounced to be immoral. There is no ambiguity whatsoever in that, especially in respect of adultery and homosexuality, which are now considered natural. I cannot decide whether those who accept both as natural are ignorant or hypocritical. It is difficult to give them even the benefit of the doubt. I find the same attitude towards abortion, which is a revolt, not simply against morality, but against biology. I, actually, consider revolt against biology to be far worse and dangerous in its consequences than the disregard of morality, because biology can do what morality cannot do—exact a terrible revenge.

There is another aspect of the rejection of traditional morality by the English people which appears to be the most bizarre of all: their calling it the rejection of Victorian morality. This is like giving a dog a bad name in order to hang it. It is exploiting the current prejudice against the Victorian age to condemn something which is timeless. Victorian morality was not a special kind of morality but only a particular form of universal morality, in no way different from morality in all ages, and as it has been from 'China to Peru'.

Thus, in regard to two of the major features of English life and civilization, I might repeat the old saying: 'Corruption of the best is the worst corruption!'

Decadence and Social Life

The most decisive impact of decadence on the social existence of the English people is to be seen in what might be regarded as its destruction or at least its undermining by bringing all individuals directly under the power and jurisdiction of the State. This has made them helpless against the power of the State.

It has also created a new function for the State, which naturally should be society's. This is to be recognized in the use of the phrase 'a caring government'. The idea has taken root that a government should take care of the people as a mother does of her baby.

On the contrary, to my thinking, it is the people's function and task to 'care' for their government by electing representatives who are best qualified to promote and safeguard national interests.

Thus the absolutism of the State, which in these days has replaced the old monarchical absolutism (without having difference in character), was bound to destroy the basic unit of society—the family, as it has been seen, not only among men, but among animals as well—that is to say, a natural grouping made up of a father (husband), a mother (wife), and their children.

I do not think that it has at any time been clearly perceived or asserted that the smallest natural unit of society is not the individual, but the family. The family is consubstantial with society, only standing in the relationship of a microcosm to a macrocosm. Truly regarded, society is a collection of families. To destroy the family is therefore to eliminate the protective barrier which absorbs the shocks of political changes or revolutions among a people.

In India, all political regimes of the past were epiphytes or even parasites on society. Society constituted the real existence of the people. Therefore, Hindu society has survived today, whereas all the past political regimes have as such left no trace whatever.

The family in its natural form was created among men and maintained by the institution of marriage. But it is this very institution which is in a shambles today. Marriage among the English people has now become a mere formal variant of a connection between a man and a woman living together outside marriage. What has become a serious and extensive attenuation of married life is its dissolution at the will of the parties, with its growing incidence. The ratio of the breakdown of marriages to their total has become almost one in three. I am surprised to see that a large number of the most distinguished persons entered in *Who's Who* have this information about their first marriage: *dissolved.*

What is more surprising is that in many cases these dissolutions are of the married couples who have remained together for decades untill both became elderly. Why did they take so long to discover that they were incompatible?

Pascal set down in an apparently cynical aphorism the cause of belated disillusionment in marriage. He said:

He no longer loves the person he loved ten years ago: She is not the same, nor is he. But perhaps he would have loved her still had she remained what she was then.

Pascal spoke only of the man. Nowadays the woman also has begun to feel the same way. That is perhaps the real feeling which brings about the end of married life today.

Thus there is being seen a new association between young men and women, which is living together outside marriage; that is, outside any religious or legal tie. Such living together was seen also in the past in England, and the participants were called Common Law husbands and wives. This sort of living has become so common nowadays that in official documents a wife has to be mentioned as a *partner*.

Along with all this there has come into existence a new type of family called a 'one-parent family'. The single parent is, of course, the mother, usually a young woman. It is even being seen that a large number of young women prefer to become unmarried mothers, because as such they are given special privileges by the government, which married women do not have. Social workers say that some of these unmarried mothers do not even know who the father, i.e. the progenitor of their child is. I have known one such woman, who could not say who was the father of her only son.

This kind of intersexual relationship has brought in two words into the English language—'boyfriend' and 'girlfriend', to mean those who were called a lover and a mistress in the old days. Even elderly men speak of their 'girlfriends', which amuses me very much. This is degrading their pretty mistresses verbally. Who does not know that old men wish to have young girls as mistresses? But it is wrong to make them cheap by depriving them of their time-honoured appellation of mistress. Decadence, however, degrades words and phrases as well as living.

I shall deal at some length with this aspect of decadence when I deal with its impact on cultural life.

Decadence, Family, and Education

The onset of decadence in England has deprived the family (in its ampler form of home) of its role in education. Till recently, the cradle of education was the home, so that education, like charity, began there. The school was to supplement that education by giving to the young people the technical knowledge of language, mathematics and other sciences which were formal accompaniments of education, without which a citizen could not maintain his civilized state. Education properly so called never included professional or vocational training; that kind of teaching was for the acquisition of skills, neither for the development of character nor for the development of intellectual power. The ancient Greeks called what I am calling real education 'Paideia'. Thus, the school was an adjunct of the home.

This relationship between the home and the school has been totally destroyed. Its place has been taken by a positive hostility of the school to the home as any kind of educational asset. The whole body of teachers in schools nowadays resents any assumption of an educational role of the family. They even threaten to expel a pupil if if it is found out that he or she is learning to read or do sums in the traditional way at home.

Yet, it has by now become clear that the methods of teaching to read or calculate followed in the schools are making the pupils incapable of reading intelligently and calculating mentally.

In respect of language, this is bringing about a shrinkage in the use of language from its widest compass to its narrowest. Language, naturally used, is something to be heard, not looked at; therefore, the visual embodiment of language is simply like a score of music, which is meaningless until it is transformed into sound in all its tones and rhythms.

In the traditional system of teaching languages, the pupils were always required to read as if they were speaking, so as to impart to what they saw as signs its full audible character.

I might add that till the nineteenth century aristocratic ladies never read themselves, they employed lectrices to read works of literature to them. Through this custom they acquired such a taste and judgement in respect of literature that they could advise even the greatest writers as to their writings. Thus the listening ladies became a powerful influence on creative literature.

This is no longer the case. Nowadays, women themselves have become writers in large numbers, but they exert no influence on the production of literature.

This has been the overall result of the impact of decadence on the literary vocation.

The home in its literacy function was called *salon*. That institution has disappeared. Even in France nobody now thinks of Madame so-and-so's Tuesday or Friday.

Decadence has Created a Young Rabble—Uine Canaille Jeune
The destruction of the traditional family with its traditional functions has led to the disappearance of the authority of the parents over their children, and the exercise of this authority to control their behaviour and activities. It seems that parents themselves no longer admit any responsibility for the actions and conduct of their children. This abandonment of responsibility of parents is seen even with their very young children, who are allowed to go out unattended to any place they like; in many cases they get lost or are found murdered. There is outcry about these incidents, but nobody asks why the children are given such freedom. Thus the misadventures of children are not tackled at their source.

An incident was recently reported in the newspapers: a little boy was awake in the living room late at night when his parents had gone to bed. He admitted robbers into the house, taking them to be expected guests and showed them where his mother kept her money hidden. Finally, he helped the robbers to carry the stolen goods to their car. This is liberation of children at its widest.

But even when there is no mishap or accident, there is complete freedom for children to go about, to behave, to act as they like. In its most undesirable form, the liberation of the youth from parental control has led to the creation of juvenile mafias which murder and rob in a professional manner. I shall consider this in the part of the book dealing with decadence in its malignant manifestations.

But even where the exercise of freedom is not criminal it approaches criminality in its extreme manifestations. For instance, young boys murder very young children out of curiosity to see what murder is like.

But generally, the least harmful exercise of freedom by young people is vandalism, disinterested and meaningless vandalism. It is mostly seen in the breaking of glass at bus shelters and damaging of seats in buses and trains.

Decadence and Cultural Life

Before I consider this matter, I must first clarify the meaning of the word 'culture'. There is a good deal of mental confusion about it. Today, its most widely intended and understood sense is not its traditional one. That was its meaning in historical works. The new meaning has come from anthropology. Writers on cultural anthropology call any distinct pattern of life of any people, civilized or primitive, culture. One of the earliest, if not the earliest, example of this is to be found in Edward Taylor's epoch-making book, *Primitive Culture,* published in 1884. Since then this usage has become the most popular meaning of the word, and by now it has driven out the old meaning, except among historians.

But I am sticking to the old meaning, and I might add that Spengler in his famous book which predicted the decline of the West regarded 'culture' as the living and creative phase of a civilization, and gave the appellation 'civilization' to its devitalized and stagnating continuation.

I got my first premonition of decay in the cultural life of the English people when I learned about the result of the general election of 1945. It gave me a shock. I now see it as having finally converted the government of the British people into a Welfare

State. No subsequent government, Conservative or Labour, has been different. Mrs Thatcher only made the Socialistic Welfare State a Capitalistic Welfare State.

I regard the Welfare State as a decadent state because I hold the considered view that mere welfare of the mass of people of a state can never restore the greatness of a people. It has been seen in respect of every country in history that its greatness as a power has had no relation with the economic prosperity or even sufficiency in the life of the majority of its people. Alexis de Tocqueville found that Napoleon held a true idea of the greatness of a people. He said that, the great genius that Napoleon was, he realized that it needed a great passion to animate the hearts of a people, and in its absence they developed a purtiscent psychological gangrene. So Napoleon, Tocqueville said, would never have wished to fix the minds of Frenchmen solely on individual well-being. Even militarism was to be preferred to that.

That is how I have now come to the final conclusion that a mere Welfare State fosters decadence, especially in the expression of national life in its culture.

With this conviction I wrote an article, which *The Daily Telegraph* published in its weekend supplement of 20 February 1988, giving it the title 'Why I Mourn for England'. Introducing the article, the editor gave this description of me:

> Today he lives in Oxford, a tiny figure, bursting with indignation for this country's mental and moral decay. It is a decay, he argues here [in the article], exemplified most tellingly in the dwindling literacy he sees around him.

By 'literacy' I really meant literary culture as a combination of knowledge and taste. I explained why a literary decline was so significant in these words:

> In England today, the public aspects of decline are tacitly admitted. There is resignation to the loss of power and wealth ... But there does not seem to be even a suspicion that decay may have penetrated the English mind, although no external decay can come about without inner decadence having set in.

I then set down what made this obvious to me. I said:

It is made manifest to me by the careless and penurious use of their language even by educated Englishmen. The human mind and human language are commensurate. So, whenever there is any decline of correctness, precision, adequacy and elegance in the use of a language there is bound to be a matching decline in the power of the mind.

What were the shortcomings in the writing of English? I answered the question in this way:

In the writing and speaking of English, grammatical strictness and precision of phrasing have virtually disappeared, making fully logical communication virtually impossible. Elegance, too, has made its exit. Above all, it is inadequacy of expression, which is seen mainly in the shrinkage of vocabulary, absence of colour in diction, and monotony of rhythm. These are serious enough to justify the assumption that the English mind, too, is losing its depth, its intensity and its capacity for making distinctions.

I saw this particularly in the changes in religious diction which were being made by the Church of England, about which I wrote in the same article:

In this [popularization of the English Bible and Prayer Book] the Anglican Church is showing a strange inconsistency. It is not making its princes give up their archaic vestments to go into jeans but putting its scriptures into a linguistic equivalent of that garment.

I gave the reason behind this incongruity in these words:

The populace have eyes to cringe to the spectacles of grand clothes, however out of date; but they do not have minds to understand traditional religious diction.

I went on to say that this popularization of diction will not save English Christianity. In all ages and among all people religion has created its diction and its hold has depended on it. Therefore, all religions have been staunchly conservative in regard to language. As long as a particular faith remains living, its special diction also remains intelligible. In Bengal, even illiterate village women understood the highly Sankritized Bengali of their sacred books. No one understands religious diction unless he is religious. The language of Christianity was never popular speech, not even in the first century of its existence. The New Testament was written in Greek, not in the natural dialect of the Jews of Palestine—Aramaic. Even the Greek was not the popular Greek of those times, but a Semitized Greek. The English Authorized Version introduced in 1611, too, was not in current Jacobean English, but was in its main diction Tudor English which was hundred years old, that of Tyndale. Popularization of religious diction then indicates religious decadence.

Secular English

It is not solely in the popularization of religious diction that a new English language is appearing today. This has become equally noticeable in what I would call the 'secular' employment of the language.

Even in the great national newspapers I read a kind of English which is not simply the English language I have been familiar with all my life but an English which I do not understand in substantial parts of it. I wondered at first whether my knowledge of English was inadequate. Then I recalled the evolution of Latin. From the second century onwards a new kind of Latin began to be used in speaking and writing by the Romans, which came to be called Vulgar, i.e. popular Latin. In course of time it supplanted classical Latin.

This historical precedent made me realize that the new English was really a Vulgar English in the manner of Vulgar Latin. But this English has not developed a homogeneous style. There have appeared styles as varied as are the fashions in women's dresses. This English is being employed by everybody—politicians, preachers, and even teachers. But its widest and most ostentatious employment is by contemporary journalists.

Today's journalese, even at its highest, is now an extraordinary mixture of colloquialism, slang, figurative diction, recondite allusions, and figures of speech, among which the most common flourishes are bad puns.

French and Spanish are also aired, but in many cases it is seen too French or Spanish by half. Let me give a French example. The journalists have taken over the French phrase *faire amour* and are using the time-honoured English phrase 'making love' as its equivalent, which it is not. The correct French equivalent of the English 'making love' is *faire la cour*. The confusion would result in a bizarre misunderstanding of Jane Austen.

Emma going home with Mr Elton in the same carriage found, 'Mr Elton actually making violent love to her'. Those who are reading English only in the newspapers today would certainly think that Mr Elton was raping Emma in the contemporary manner. Jane Austen, however, only meant that he was professing 'ardent attachment', 'unexampled passion' and 'adoration'.

This is, of course, only one of the examples of the degradation of time-honoured English words, like sex and gay. The phrase 'fair sex' would certainly be drastically misunderstood today.

The impact of decadence on the journals of today is also seen in the headlines given to news reports. These are made as sensational as possible in order to redeem the dullness that follows. But I say wickedly that those who need such headlines to be induced to read the news are exactly like those who need aphrodisiacs to perform the sexual act naturally.

Impact of Decadence on the English Personality

The impact of decadence has not remained confined to language; it has spread to the English personality, changing it in many ways. I shall mention the more important changes in the outlook on life of the English people in a series.

(a) Race- and Colour-consciousness: The Englishman in the past was notoriously contemptuous of all foreigners, and of coloured people insultingly so. The general body of Englishmen in India called even Indians 'Niggers', and extenuated their murder by themselves on that ground, so that Lord Curzon as Viceroy of India was provoked to indignant protest. He recognized that: 'When a haughty race like the English rule Asiatic peoples like Indians, incidents of *hubris* and violence will occur.' Even so, he declared, he would not be a party to 'the theory that a white man may kick or batter a black man to death with impunity because he is only "a d–d nigger".' Lord Salisbury as Prime Minister described Dadabhai Naoroji, an MP and as fair as an Italian, as a 'Black Man'.

But contemporary Englishmen declare that they have changed all that. A vocal and influential minority are saying that the immigration of coloured people will enrich English life by making it multilingual and multicultural. Today, apparently, the distinction between the words adulteration and enrichment has ceased to be recognized.

This change of attitude in Englishmen has evoked a strange response from the coloured party. I have received a prospectus (perhaps because I am supposed to be black) which announces the establishment of a prize called Saga, of the value of £3,000, to any 'Black writer born in Britain or in the Republic of Ireland'. Never before was I aware that writers could be classified as 'white' or 'black'. As a writer in English I have even refused to be classed as an 'Indian writer'. I declared publicly when I was in India that when I write in English I am a 'writer in India', not an 'Indian writer'. I hold the view that writers should be classified only by the language they write in and not by country, race, or complexion.

(b) The Hard Core of Racial and Colour Prejudice in England: Yet, racial arrogance and colour prejudice have not disappeared among the English people. Both remain in the marrow of their bones. This is felt, to my knowledge, by all Indians who hold high positions in administration, industry, or even universities, perhaps most keenly in the last. Most of them have become anxious about the tenure of their posts.

I can say in a general way that an Indian has to possess at least twice the competence of an Englishman in order to have equality of recognition with his or her English colleagues. One general rule about the effect of decadence on any people is that it always weakens their good qualities, but leaves the bad ones as they were.

(c) We Must Not Praise Our Great Men: Here one finds a total reversal of attitude, which is an accompaniment of decadence. It transforms history into biography in order to make people read it. The traditional and popular view of history was put by Jane Austen in the mouth of Catherine Morland in *Northanger Abbey*. Catherine said when she heard that her friend Miss Tilney read history:

> You are fond of history! And so are Mr Allen and my father and I have two brothers who do not dislike it. So many instances within my small circle of friends is remarkable! At this rate, I shall not pity the writers of history any longer. If people like to read their books, it is all very well, but to be at so much trouble in filling great volumes, which, as I used to think, nobody would willingly ever look into, to be labouring only for the torment of little boys and girls, always struck me as a hard fate ... I have often wondered at the person's courage that could sit down one purpose to do it.

But history written as biography would give it the interest which men and women feel in their fellowmen, especially if they are or were famous, and even more so if the biographies give more attention to the weaknesses of their subjects than to their good qualities. Nothing has more piquant appeal than scandal-mongering about great men.

This was seen in the case of the Roman biographer, Snetonius, who wrote history as biography, and even biography as scandal-mongering. He wrote in the third century, which saw the onset of decadence in Roman life.

This kind of scandal-mongering even represented Faustina, wife of Marcus Aurelius, as a loose woman, and Commodus a bastard, in spite of his striking resemblance to his father, Marcus Aurelius.

Popularity of this kind of biographical scandal-mongering made even Procopius, a serious historian of the reign of Justinian, supplement his 'open' work of history by his 'secret history'. In it, Empress Theodora was exposed as the most shameless harlot in her young days as a dancer.

These ancient precedents are being followed by contemporary English biographers. I say rather flippantly that the most serious concern of present-day English biographers seems to be to find out whether their subject is a bastard or a bugger. They think, if they can find their subject to be one or the other, they would deprive him of his greatness, which they resent. But they overlook how irrelevant is this inquiry to the greatness of a ruler. They seem to have forgotten that the most illustrious 'bastard' in history was William the Conqueror, the founder of the English State.

A man with the weaknesses of a decadent would naturally try to show that no great man of the past was better than he is. They exclaim like Beatrix in Thackeray's novel *Henry Esmond* when her mother reminds her of her father: *'Eh mon père*, was no better than other persons' fathers.'

I do not think I have to expatiate on the spirit of the contemporary biographical historians. Their inducements and inspirations come from decadence.

I think this 'debunking' of their great men has come to colour the popular view of them. In this connection I shall quote a remark of Chateaubriand in my translation.

> How foolish is the man who believes in history, which is pure deception. It remains what a great writer has coloured and fashioned it. When it will be found from monographs which demonstrate with clear evidence that what Tacitus only retailed fakes in describing the virtues of Agricola and the vices of Tiberius, Agricola and Tiberius will remain what Tacitus made them.
>
> (Essai sur la literature anglaise (1836), see Scènes et Portraits Historianes entraits de l'Oeuvre de Chateaubriand. Librarie Plan 1933, p. 269)

Only, the present-day historians are not comparable to Tacitus. He was inspired by indignation, the modern biographers are driven only by rancour and malice.

(d) Decline of Sensibility: Last of all, I shall single out among the many harmful effects of decadence on the human personality that which I consider to be the most serious one. It is the erosion of all delicate sensibilities, normal in civilized men and women.

This is being brought about mainly by the audio-visual providers of entertainment through TV and similar electronic devices. I shall say that in playing this mischievous role the BBC is showing itself to be the most enterprising. Those who make TV features for it have become incapable of understanding the English fiction they draw on. I hold very strongly that audio-visual exploitation of literature has become the most effectual means of destroying literary culture among the English people. I meet very few people who can now say that they have read the original novels shown as TV features. It is perfectly legitimate for the providers of visual entertainment to tell any story audio-visually, provided they make an original art form of it. But they do not do that exclusively. Most often they take their stories from famous novels, the more famous the better. Thus, these audio-visual stories become epiphytes or parasites of literary stories, and substantially distort and misrepresent them.

I have noticed this most often in the BBC's treatment of Jane Austen, whose intention and spirit the producers seem to be incapable of understanding. They transform Jane Austen into somebody whom I cannot recognize as Jane Austen, whom I began to read in 1914 and have been reading almost every day.

Let me illustrate by taking the latest rendering of *Pride and Prejudice*, which has been acclaimed as a stunning feat.

In the scene in which Elizabeth accepts Darcy with pleasure and gratitude after having rejected his offer with scorn and anger six months before, the new presentation makes Elizabeth kiss Darcy on the mouth. This has even been reproduced in the newspapers.

But how did Jane Austen herself describe the incident? Here it is:

> The happiness which this reply [acceptance of Darcy's proposal] produced was shown as he [Darcy] had probably never felt before, and he expressed himself on the occasion as sensibly and as warmly as a man violently in love can be supposed to do.

Jane Austen continues: *'Had Elizabeth been able to encounter his eye*, she might have seen how well the expression of heart-felt delight, diffused over his face, became him' (italics mine).

The same reserve in describing acceptance of love by young girls was shown by Balzac and George Sand, who could not be regarded as being ignorant of the physical side of the man–woman relationship.

I would only add that such was the natural behaviour of all girls in all countries so long as delicacy of feeling was a trait of their

101

personalities. I might also refer to what Jane Austen made Elizabeth feel when her younger sister Lydia (according to her 'at sixteen the most determined flirt that ever made herself and her family ridiculous, a flirt too in the worst and meanest degree of flirtation'), said about another girl: 'Who could care about such a nasty little freckled thing?'

This is Elizabeth's reaction to Lydia's speech, as shown by Jane Austen:

> Elizabeth was shocked to think that, however incapable of such coarseness of *expression* herself, the coarseness of the *sentiment* was little other than her own breast had formerly harboured.

Of course, in decadence such delicacy cannot be expected. In fact, in an age of decadence even respect for delicacy disappears.

One day, a young English woman, who was making a TV feature with me at Oxford for the BBC told me contemptuously, when suddenly and somehow Jane Austen's *Mansfield Park* came into the talk: 'I don't like Fanny.' Of course, she would not; could anyone making TV features for the BBC?

Malignant Features of English Decadence

Here I am going to describe the malignant side of the English decadence, as I find it reported in the newspapers. There can be no doubt that in Britain crimes of the most horrifying and degraded character are being committed in ever greater numbers, and with increasing atrocity. Since I am by implication laying the blame for all this on the 'English people', I feel I ought to make clear whom I have in mind. I wish to meet in advance the admonition: 'You cannot indict a whole people.'

Of course, that is true. But a people as a whole may be blameless without a portion of them not being so. Nations are not homogeneous in their mental identity. Among them, some may be active, some passive; some thoughtful, some thoughtless; some introspective, some totally extrovert. As a rule, the greater majority of any nation are passive and thoughtless. They follow the established way of life of the nation and never think of even examining it, not to speak of questioning it.

But their passivity is like the so-called 'cold blood' of reptiles. That only means the absence in their metabolism of the capacity to keep the temperature of the blood at a warm normal. But the blood temperature of all reptiles changes with the ambient temperature in the atmosphere. If the blood temperature of a snake makes it feel uncomfortable, it seeks the cool of its hole.

In the same way, the moral awareness of the passive masses of a nation may be roused or deadened by the moral trends current in society. However they might be created, they are imposed by an assertive minority, who are dominant for the time being. Thus the passive majority can be made responsible only in their submission to the dominant minority. As a rule, they submit.

So, if I speak of the criminality of the 'English people' I mean that of the assertive minority and their coalescence with the derivative criminality of the masses. To that extent the latter are 'criminal'. I leave the question of the responsibility for the crimes that are being perpetrated in Britain today at that.

But there is an aspect of the passive acquiescence of the masses which cannot be overlooked. It is the prevalence of sympathy for criminals, on an assumption that they are not less sinned against than sinning. This leads an impartial observer to suspect the presence of a criminal 'libido' in the masses, which makes them vicariously criminal. This inclination has been poetically described by Baudelaire in these lines:

Si le n'ol, le poison, le poignard, l' incendie
N'ont pas encarbrodé' de leurs plaisants dessins
Le canvas banal de nos piteux destins,
C'est que notre âme, hélas! n'est as assez hardie.

[If rape, poison, dagger, incendiarism have not as yet embroidered the banal canvas of our piteous destinies with their pleasant designs, that is because our heart, alas! is not bold enough.]

I am sure, the *Hugo-helás*! was a mischievous prank of Baudelaire's.

But this sympathy for criminals has also an insidiously danger-ous implication. It appears with the loss of vitality in a nation, which always engenders a repulsive moral turpitude, making crimes al-most a normal form of social self-assertion. Then it acquires the character of cancerous malignancy. I am convinced that the English people have reached that state or at all events are approaching it.

There is yet another point to clear up about the criminality of the English people—that is to find out who or what is responsible for it. It is usually attributed to the scenes of violence exhibited on TV. That, to my thinking, is a fallacy. TV shows scenes of violence as the purveyors of 'consumer goods'. It meets a demand, although it also increases the demand by fostering the taste.

In regard to this, the illogicality is the same as what is being shown in dealing with drug addiction. There, too, it is the dealers in drugs who are being punished. Nobody considers that the drug trade has been made profitable only by the addicts. Why do they appear in society and among the wealthiest class? But to deal with them is difficult. The cause of widespread drug addiction is impos-sible to discover. It is one of those social trends which are so mysterious that they seem to appear as the wind blows. No historian has been able to account for such trends.

I think this lengthy explanation will protect me against any suspicion that in giving the account of criminality in Britain I have a bias or preconceived notion. But I will also say that even though I shall not give expression to my horror, I shall remain horrified.

Now for my account of the crimes among the English people. It will be systematic and, so far as I can make it so, colourless.

(a) The most serious, but not the most atrocious, crime is armed robbery on banks and post-offices. Theft is now a very petty offence, and is even being regarded as a permissible if regrettable satisfaction of the acquisitive urge of people unjustly frustrated in respect of this.

Robberies have compelled banks and post-offices to erect bar-riers of bulletproof plateglass screens between the depositors and the receivers at the counters, making personal contact impossible. In addition, narrow receptacles are now provided for paying and receiving money, and in them fingers of the payers and receivers can never be in contact.

Even so the robberies are still being perpetrated, and the robbers are showing increasing finesse.

(b) Robberies on private homes are more serious socially, for they are often accompanied by murder. The robbers usually carry sawed-off shotguns and use them if resisted. The most significant feature of these robberies is not the money, but the lives lost.

If a householder uses arms against robbers he has to justify it; otherwise he is prosecuted for murder. There is no unlimited right of self-defence.

The most atrocious feature of such robberies is that they are often on lone elderly women. The robbers, especially young robbers, regard them as the easiest targets.

Equally significant is the fact that young robbers are increasing in numbers. Sometimes they are not older than twelve or thirteen.

(c) The most significant crime not connected with money is murder from various motives. These are committed by husbands on wives and also by wives on husbands either for obtaining freedom for extra-marital affairs, or from provocation given by ill-treatment. A case was recently reported of a husband drowning his wife in a bath, and then spending the rest of the night with his mistress.

(d) Murders are also being committed from irrational homicidal mania. Incidents of such murders are becoming frequent, and I shall have more to say about the most horrifying of such murders.

(e) Rape, certainly the most unnatural performance of the sexual act, is taking two forms, which makes it even more unnatural and atrocious, viz. being perpetrated on very young girls, even of six or seven and on old women; what is even more horrifying is that rape nowadays is almost always accompanied by murder of the raped girl or woman. This particular crime has become so common that the police are advising young women not to go out unaccompanied after dark. Very young girls are abducted even when they are near their homes, and their naked bodies are later found hidden in a bush. Taking a lift from a stranger has become taking the risk of being raped, or raped and murdered.

(f) Juvenile crime, not in any way a less serious aggravation of criminality among the English people, is seen in its extension to young boys, even young boys of twelve. They murder or rape out of sheer curiosity to see what these are like. The legal doctrine of absence of moral responsibility under a certain age protects these young criminals, although the same doctrine does not protect dogs.

(g) Another manifestation of malignant decadence concerns babies. Young women who want a child steal a newborn baby even from maternity hospitals; slightly older babies are stolen from prams left outside by shopping mothers.

There is also killing of babies by unmarried mothers who do not want to further burden themselves after bearing the burden during pregnancy. Therefore, they abandon them or kill them.

In former days unmarried mothers felt compelled to bring up their children of love, sometimes representing them as nephews or nieces. Kipling wrote a story about the latter kind. These children grew up to lead the lines of ordinary persons and nobody was too particular about their fathers. The son of an unmarried mother even became Prime Minister of England. I assume that educated Englishmen know who he was.

I am writing about the crimes of malignant decadence in a matter-of-fact manner as if they were like the everyday activities of ordinary men and women in a law-abiding and civilized society, such as going out for a walk or to shop. In writing in such a manner I am only imitating the indifference with which people nowadays view the crimes. When these become as common as they are now, the general public accepts them as all in a day's work. Otherwise, they would go mad with fury. Decadence always provides its anaesthetics.

But I shall not be able to affect this indifference in taking note of a kind of crime which is unprecedented in the history of all previous ages of decadence: massacre of young children.

(h) There was such an outrage at Hungerford in 1987, which led to the adoption of some preventive measures like restriction of licences for firearms. But these have not been able to prevent another massacre whose atrocious character could not be envisaged even in a nightmare.

On 13 March 1996, shortly after nine o'clock, a man of forty-three, T.W. Hamilton, burst into a primary school at Dunblane near Stirling (Scotland) and began firing with automatic weapons on children exercising in the gymnasium of the school. All the children were five-year-olds. Fifteen of them died immediately, and also their teacher. One child died subsequently in hospital. After killing the children Hamilton shot himself.

It is impossible to give any rational explanation of the man's behaviour. He had been nursing a sense of grievance for over ten years, and it had been growing keener, as it does if it cannot be got rid of by strength of character. This may have led him at last to perpetrate that horrible massacre from the motive of avenging his wrongs. But why did he kill himself instead of living to enjoy his revenge? He knew that he would not be hanged for his crime, but only kept in prison. Did he then, after committing his crime, feel any prick of conscience? It is impossible to explain the working of his mind. But taken in itself, his crime remains the only one in the whole history of civilized man in respect of cruelty. It showed to what level even deliberate murder could sink.

But in the days following the massacre, I was surprised to read the explanations of this crime given by highly educated men in the light of the Christian belief in an Absolute Evil, personified in Satan as the rival of God. 'Our school was visited by Evil' was one full-page headline.

To my thinking, there is no doctrine more mistaken and more likely to misdirect moral sensibility than that of shifting responsibility from human beings to an imagined personification of Evil. I thought I was seeing a repetition of the extenuation of crime which had been long-standing in Europe. As if that was not enough, on 17 March I read a pronouncement from the Archbishop of Canterbury that churchgoers should think of Hamilton as their brother and understand the pressures that drove Thomas Hamilton to kill.

I was struck down, almost physically, by this preaching of Christian charity by the latest successor of St Augustine and St

Anselm. This Archbishop of Canterbury certainly wanted to give the impression of being noble enough to forgive even such a criminal.

And it is certainly a paradox created by decadence that a heathen Hindu like me should remind the highest dignitary of the Church of England that there is in Christianity also a belief in the wrath of God. I am compelled to assume that the Archbishop has not read even the New Testament, e.g. this passage in it:

> He that overcometh shall inherit all things; and I will be his God, and he shall be my son.
>
> But the fearful, and unbelieving, and abominable, and murderers, and whoremongers and sorcerers, and idolaters, and all liars, shall have their part in the lake which burneth with fire and brimstone which is the second death.
>
> (The Revelation of St John the Divine, 21: 7–8

It also seems that he has never read the famous hymn given in a free translation in hymn no. 398 in the Book of Common Prayer of the Anglican Church.

> Dies irae, dies illa
> Solvet saeclum in favilla ...
>
> (Analecta Hymnica, liv, p. 269)

The exercise of Christian charity by the latest successor of St Augustine reminds me of a resounding biblical pronouncement which I quote in the comparative obscurity of Latin:

> Cum autem videritis
> abominationem desolationis stantem
> ubi non debet, qui legit, intelligat tunc qui in Indàea sunt ...

So, even if you did not wish to flee England after the massacre, you will perhaps do so after the preaching of Christian charity by the successor of St Augustine.

Chapter 3

Decadence in India

It will be far easier for me to write about decadence in India than it has been in the case of England. I was prepared for decadence in my country, not only by my reading of Indian history, but also by a feeling of discomfort when I entered the world in 1921, after leaving the University of Calcutta.

In India there had been two previous periods of decadence: the first for about two hundred years before the Muslim conquest at the end of the twelfth century; the second, in the eighteenth century, after the death of the last great Mogul emperor Aurangzeb. The first decadence brought about the extinction of the ancient Hindu civilization; the second, of the Indo-Islamic.

With this knowledge of history, I felt in 1921 that certain essential features of our cultural life up to my young days were disappearing and certain trends which had not been seen before were making their appearance. The latter went on gaining ground until they swamped the old life by 1947. Then I recognized what had happened and wrote about it in the first part of my autobiography. The passages were written at the end of 1947 although the book was published in 1951. I shall quote these:

> In our national life the period of my manhood, except for one or two short interludes, was devoid of colour and charged with tedium. Thus it could hardly be called duration. In those years time seemed to have became spatialized, transformed into a lagoon which could still break into ripples, but which none the less was dead, because it was completely cut off from all living currents.

Then followed my realization.

My First Diagnosis of Decadence

I wrote:

> Yet even in its stagnancy the thing was not immune from an evil metamorphosis. Those who kept their eyes fixed only on the watery surface did not detect this morbid change. They found it still capable of glimmering under the sun and the moon, and failed to perceive how low the water was falling.
>
> But those who were alert could detect at the edges, first a dark line, then a ring, after that a ribbon, next a belt, and lastly, broad patches of black, and wake up with a start to the realization that the wretched thing was drying and converting itself into a mud-flat. Something worse that even its sickly self.

I regarded that as decadence in 1947, and I did not do so without carefully considering what the word meant. As I wrote:

> As far back as 1922 I received a warning from Mr Middleton Murry's book *The Problem of Style* not to employ the word 'decadence' too readily and lightly. I was taught to redouble this caution by Rémy de Gourmont, to whom Mr Murry had referred his readers. So I do not make use of the word without weighing every shade of its meaning.

Then I summed up my diagnosis of decadence in India, as it had been set down by me in 1947. Here it is:

> What I am speaking about is true decadence, for during those years everything about us was decaying, literally everything ranging from our spiritual and moral ideals to our material culture, and nothing really live or organic arose to take their place. I have never even read about such a process as I have passed through: it was unadulterated decadence.
>
> (*The Autobiography of an Unknown Indian;* first English edition, 1951, p. 364)

In the second part of my autobiography, which covered the years from 1921 to 1952 and was entitled *Thy Hand, Great Anarch!* and was published in 1987, on my ninetieth birthday, I described

110

the whole process. I summed up what I saw in a quotation from Pope's *Dunciad:*

> Lo! thy dread Empire, Chaos! is restor'd;
> Light dies before thy uncreating word;
> Thy hand, great Anarch! Lets the curtain fall
> And Universal Darkness buries All!'

Even so, I did not expect that I should have to add to my story of Indian decadence. I now find that descent is endless, as Virgil with his uncanny prescience wrote:

> Facilis descensus Averno:
> Noctes at que dies patet atri
> Lanna Ditis.
>
> [Easy is the descent to the underworld; by night and day the door of dark Dis stands open.]

So, I have to take the story of Indian decadence further. The sole relieving feature in it is that it does not exhibit the malignity which is seen in England. It is only a comatose senility, in which India is hearing a repetition of the saying: Growing old is really—

> To hear the world applaud the
>   *hollow ghost*
> Which blamed the living man.

That is why I fear the *White Man*, especially when he brings us presents, above all—eulogium.

Premonition of Decadence: On the Eve

Even before the decision to leave India was taken, I felt sure that it was coming. So I sent a note to the editor of *The New English Review* about what was seen in India after the disappearance of Mogul political power and before British rule was established. The hint throughout was that those conditions might be seen in the coming imperial interregnum. The note was published in the December 1946 issue of the magazine. I quote the whole of it:

111

(1) Complete ineffectiveness of the state: It could not resist foreign invasion, put down internal rebellions, suppress Hindu–Muslim riots [there were Hindu–Muslim riots even in those days], could not ensure efficient administration, and was not successful in any project it initiated. One rebel (at Allahabad, Pandit Nehru's domicile) dictated the name of the imperial representative who would be a *persona grata* to him and with whom he would negotiate. He demanded the costs of his rebellion and got them, and also a new governorship as a quid pro quo for his submission. In the imperial camp drums were beaten in honour of this victory.

(2) Concessions were made and accepted with mental reservations as a matter of expediency and not as a matter of principle. Sometimes the opportunism went as far as downright dishonesty where both sides had no other design but to doublecross each other. Scores of such instances may be cited.

(3) The ineffectiveness was due primarily to the exhaustion of Muslim political power (both inside and outside India). But a secondary and not unimportant cause was 'Indianization', that is to say, installation of Hindus (particularly of the *Bania* class) and Indianized Muslims in positions where, instead of being subordinates, they could influence policy. The spirit of the administration was altered and the vigour gone with the decline of the Turkish and Persian elements.

(4) Political life and state service came to be regarded as the means of promoting private interests alone, and all posts were filled by careerists. The public revenues were looked upon as legitimate loot, and through jobbery and wire-pulling the careerists could get almost any assignment they wanted on the public revenues.

(5) The Marathas and the Congress have suggestively similar characteristics. The Marathas were impelled by two motive forces: first, the negative xenophobia (especially Muslimophobia) of the Hindus, and, secondly, the mercenary motive of plunder and exaction. Of the two social orders on which the power of the Congress rests, the Hindu professional middle-class supplies the first and the *Bania* class the second. The Congress resembles the Marathas in the sterility, lack of originality, and imitativeness of its political ideas.

(6) The effect of the decline of the State on the masses was twofold. One section took to loot, murder, robbery, and finally evolved into the

Pindari, while the other simply ran away into the jungles at the slightest sign of trouble.

(7) Lastly, there grew up a habit of tolerance of anarchy and corruption, or at all events resignation to them. It was not till the British power re-established order that people again looked upon peace and security as something to which they were entitled by birthright. That murder, arson, plunder, bribes, peculation are not normal is a sense which is becoming increasingly numb in modern India.

(Reproduced in *They Hand, Great Anarch!* pp. 859–60)

Written in 1946, that was not, I would say, an inaccurate prognosis.

Aspects and Stages of Political Decadence in India

The most striking aspect of government in India after the gift of independence by the British people was its total falsity. Nothing was authentic, nothing sincere, nothing disinterested in it. Instead of showing fear of this gift from white men, all Indians exulted over it. Those who took over the business of governing India proved the truth of the saying: 'Patriotism is the last refuge of a scoundrel.'

Yet, the man who on the day of independence became virtually the dictator of India, was *not* himself a scoundrel or even a counterfeit. He was wholly genuine, as an Englishman of radical views. But he was not endowed with practical political capacity. As soon as with independence he abandoned his former role of demagogue, he became an ineffable idéologue, flapping his wings against the bars of the cage in which he was put by the bureaucracy. The political programme which he himself wished to put into effect was to make India a Soviet Union in technology, and a parliamentary democracy in governance. He alone did not realize that he was really a dictator without the will to exercise his dicta-torial power. I said so publicly in an article published when he was living.

But just as he would not act like a dictator, he could not also become a practical democratic statesman. He took refuge in escap-ism. He shunned all policies and actions in which he knew he would have to face the massive stability of the Indian masses and the cunning self-seeking of the professional politicians of his party. He began to build national structures like dams with the help of American engineers and public buildings with the help of Le Corbusier. His object was to bypass all realities in India. I called these material structures the pyramids of Nehru; alas! not as long-lasting as those at Gizah.

So, the task of actually governing and legislating India passed to the officials and Congress politicians, both of whom were hard-boiled opportunists and adventurers, the most hard-boiled to be seen anywhere in the world.

Another natural inclination of Nehru's, which was created by his entire upbringing and education by an English tutor at home, and at Harrow and Cambridge later, was that he would not employ anybody who was not educated abroad, especially at Cambridge or Oxford. As all Indians so educated were, as a class, pure opportunists who only pursued self-interest, he got a whole cohort of them round himself. His political colleagues he was compelled to accept as the unavoidable company imposed on him by the new universal franchise. But he would not accept them as fellow-workers. He got together those who were educated abroad. This made him select as his highest adviser on foreign policy Sir Girija Shanker Bajpai, a member of the Indian Civil Service, who under the British had carried on active propaganda against the Congress in the United States. But at least he was a decent and refined opportunist. Most of the others whom he selected for important jobs were malodorous like skunks. Thus India under Nehru government was like castles in Spain resting on kitchens if not sewers.

I assumed that this unnatural government could not last in India and the power of the Anglicized Indian would disappear with Nehru's death, which in any case could not be far distant. At that time I was asked by a very important journal in India to write an article on the question: After Nehru, Who? Instead of hazarding a guess, I said that 'After Nehru, What?' was the crucial question and not 'Who'. My assumption did not prove to be correct. The dictatorship of the Nehru dynasty continued with short interruptions, which were like the 'accidentals' in a musical composition. The normal key was quickly restored.

Its restoration as intended by those who brought in the new government in 1967, was to instal a figurehead to their government. Instead it produced the opposite result. In making Indira Gandhi, the sweet and gracious daughter of Nehru, Prime Minister of India, they caught a Tartar. The position brought about a transformation in Mrs Gandhi's character paralleled only by the promising Ivan Romanov's becoming Ivan the Terrible. The Indian Boyars were routed.

Mrs Gandhi's sole preoccupation was to remain in office and in power by foiling the hydra-headed opposition to her in a faction-ridden political world. This made her resort to such unscrupulous yet imprudent manoeuvres that she was murdered by agents of the fanatical Akali Sikhs.

Even her murder did not put an end to dynastic rule. Her son became Prime Minister and continued it. But his imprudent policy with regard to Sri Lanka made him a victim to a woman suicide bomber. As things have turned out, it seems dynastic rule in India has finally come to an end. But what has followed it?

The Present Regime*

The answer is simple: the inevitable consequences of the disappearance of personal rule in Indian political life has been seen to be rule by a faction or an opportunistic combination of many factions.

But it is now a very exceptional kind of factional government. During the period of Mogul rule there were three factions at the court—the Turani or Turkish, the Irani or Persian, or Hindustani, Indian—all Muslims, of course. At present there are numerous factions all over India and all with separate vested interests. So it is very difficult to combine them even in opportunistic collaboration.

At present, there is a very broad line of separation, viz. between the factions in the Indo-Gangetic plain, or Hindustan, or Aryavarta on the one hand; and on the other, the factions from the peripheral

---

*This was written when the Narasimha Rao government was in power.

provinces. But the present government in India is dominantly government by politicians from the Deccan. The present Prime Minister is a Telugu-speaking Brahmin from the Andhra region. His colleagues are also either from the Deccan or isolated politicians in the north. The north as a whole is the Opposition today.

This has brought about an ideological division in the government of India: the north standing for Hindu nationalism, and the south for what is represented as secular and liberal government. This distinction has in its turn made the government in office a replica, an *ersatz* replica, of British government in India in its last three decades, and the politicians of north India a contemporary Indian National Congress. So, just as in the last decades of British rule Indian politics was only a contest between British rule and the nationalists, at present it is an opposition between a government in office which is exactly like the British government in India and an Opposition which is the old Congress in its latest form.

I wrote an article on this peculiar political situation in India in 1994. It was published in *The Statesman* of Calcutta under the title 'British Rule is Dead, Long Live British Rule!', which was an adaptation of the French cry on the death of one autocratic king and the succession of another autocratic ruler. It simply meant that even if a particular monarch passed away, the monarchy remained: that is to say, only the person disappears, but not the institution.

By adapting this saying to the Indian political situation, I wanted to say that what disappeared from India with the going away of the British was only the white personnel, but the system of government the British had created remained, intact in all its features and above all in its spirit. The present government of India is pursuing policies, especially in regard to the so-called minorities, which in British days used to be defined by the phrase: *Divide et impera.*

But it must not be assumed that my perception of the continuation of British rule in India after independence dates only from the end of the Nehru dynasty; it dawned on me with the very inauguration of independence, when I had not realized that Nehru was to create a dynasty. So, I wrote in the article for *The Statesman*:

The immense noisy crowds that greeted the end of British rule in India with deafening shouts of joy on August 15, 1947, did not recall the old saying; they thought nothing of British rule would survive in their country after the departure of the White men who had carried it on. They never perceived that British rule in India had created an impersonal structure ... a system of government for which there was no substitute.

In this system, the actual work of government was carried on by a bureaucracy consisting of the highest British officials together with a hierarchy of officials whose lowest but the most numerous personnel was formed by the clerks. Actual initiation of government action was in the hands of the men in the lowest position, viz. the clerks.

Lord Curzon was infuriated by this system but failed to remove it. It kept its hold, and around 1924, Field-Marshal Lord Rawlinson, who was Commander-in-Chief in India, wrote in his diary:

> The chief weakness of India today is that she is caught in the net of Babuism—which she had herself created during long years of parochial and pedantic administration. She is hampered on all sides by precedents, vested interests, and ancient customs.

What Lord Rawlinson had in mind was a system of government in which initiative had to surge to the highest level from the lowest level and execution had to seep down to the lowest from the highest, and since the lowest level of the government at first was composed of Bengali clerks, he used the word 'Babuism'.

In the same article I described the basic character of the Indian bureaucracy as it is now in these words:

> Theirs is a solid, egocentric, and rootless order, which by its very nature, is not only uncreative, but even unproductive. Its only purpose is to perpetuate itself by inbreeding, and ensure its prosperity.

Government by such a bureaucracy can by itself be regarded as a decisive sign of decadence of a people in their political life. But in India it has been taken further down by making the 'dealing clerk' the initiator of the motive force of all action by the government. The 'dealing clerk' by taking leave of absence or even by his truancy can stop governmental action. If this is the *reductio ad absurdum* of government, it is also making decadence in respect of government triumphant. This decadence no longer has to be militant.

Social and Cultural Decadence

I have now to complete my account of decadence in India by describing its expansion into social and cultural life, and, of course, as its inescapable accompaniment—decadence of mental life.

During the periods of Hindu and Muslim rule, political regimes in India had no organic relationship with the general life of the people. They only superimposed an exploitative, almost predatory, class of men on the people; this class maintained law and order only to the extent that this was necessary for full-scale exploitation. They would not permit the infringement of their monopoly of robbery.

Thus the historical political regimes of ancient Hindu India left no trace or memory of their existence among the people. Before the European Orientalists discovered the historical ancient India, the Indian people knew nothing of Chandragupta and Asoka and the Maurya dynasty, of Chandragupta, Samudragupta and the Gupta dynasty, of Harsha, of the Palas of Bengal, the Pratiharas of upper India, and the Rashtrakutas of the Deccan. The entire historic Hindu rule left only two names, Vikramaditya and Bhoja-Raja, to be applied to any great ruler. For the rest, the legends embodied in the two epics, the Ramayana and the Mahabharata, became the only sources of the political life of ancient Hindus. Rama's rule was the Hindu Pax Britannica, and the conflict between the Kurus and the Pandavas the civil war par excellence.

The Muslims, in contrast, brought historical knowledge and memory to India, but this did not create a political life which impinged on the life of the people. They brought into existence only a lasting relationship between the ruling order and the general mass of the people created by Muslim rule through the system of revenue collection introduced during the reign of the Mogul emperor Akbar by his Punjabi Khatri revenue minister, Todar Mal.

So it was left for British rule to establish a close relationship between the political regime in India and the Indian people. That was created especially by the creation of a Hindu official class and a Hindu professional class. Through them the political order and the social order became intertwined, and on account of this any changes in the political order were bound to produce corresponding changes in the life of the people. Thus the decadence of political life in India had its counterpart in the decadence in social and cultural life, although there were also trends towards decadence innate in those areas of life.

I shall now give a summary account of the social and cultural decadence without distinguishing between its causes.

General Character of the Social and Cultural Decadence in India

On the whole, it resembles the decadence in England in these spheres, but there are differences which either intensify or weaken the manifestations in India. At the same time, its visible manifestations are more American than English. The most conspicuous outward manifestation of social and cultural decadence in India is the popular and lowest expression of Americanism. This is also inducing many enterprising Indians to emigrate and settle in the United States, so as to be in their real cultural home. But there they join only that element of the American population which is composed of its 'sansculottes'. When I was for a time professor in the University of Texas at Austin, we entertained in the manner of the professors there. When a fellow-Indian saw my wife's table he laughed and said: 'What have you done? People here would laugh at you.' Yet the China was Lennox.

Particular Features of the Social and Cultural Decadence in India

I can now proceed,to describe the particular features of the Indian decadence, and I shall begin with:

(a) Money-making. This is more single-minded, sordid, and dishonest in India than in England, and this debasement of the pursuit of money marks it as a manifestation of decadence. The traditional Hindu orders had always a place in it for resolute money-making to the exclusion of all other interests. That was practised by the castes or classes to whom the Hindu sacred law (Dharmasastra) assigned the 'social duty' of providing wealth for the entire order. So, for these castes and classes money-making was a vocation rather than a profession; the special characterization of it in Sanskrit was dedication to *svadharma*. There still survive in India money-makers of this type. Most of the Indian immigrants in England who have become fabulously wealthy are families of that type. So are the Hindu retailers at a less wealthy level.

The Islamic order, too, provided an honourable place for its traders. It never created any social distinction between the gentry and the tradesmen which was seen in England. Whether in Cairo, Baghdad, or Delhi the shop was as honoured a place as a castle or a country house.

But in the last few decades there has appeared in India a new upstart class of money-makers who surpass the English money-makers in sordidness and dishonesty. It is this new-rich class which is contributing to social decadence in India.

(b) Licentiousness. In this sphere decadence is showing less degradation in India than in England and is not becoming a force for destroying the family. This is due to the fact that traditional Hindu society provided a wide scope for licentiousness within family relationships as a safety valve. The only restriction imposed on licentiousness was that it should be secret, always assumed but never paraded. This makes the licentiousness which is now being seen in India less significant than that which is rampant in England. Furthermore, licentiousness has not become dogmatic in India. It is only an easing of the rigour of social inhibition.

But it is acquiring a social character, coming out of its familial segregation. This is due to two new developments in Hindu social life: first, the virtual disappearance of the purdah system and unrestricted meeting of men and women; secondly, the new Hindu law of divorce. Formerly, there was informal separation between husband and wife arising from incompatibility, but no formal divorce. Now, for young Hindu wives the husband's friend has potentially acquired the new attribute of a lover, and that without becoming a co-respondent in a divorce case but only being the tacit cause of it. I am told that the man–woman relationship among educated Indians is drifting perceptively towards Western practice. But I know that over this question there may be both exaggeration and understatement—in India perhaps exaggeration on account of its open exhibition. I shall leave the consideration of licentiousness as a feature of Indian decadence at that.

(c) Mores. There are three aspects of the *mores* or the *nonos* of a people which indicate its soundness or unsoundness, its vitality or loss of vitality, and its authenticity or its falsity. These are speech, dressing and eating. These go together, and if there is absence of strictness in one, there will be the same absence in the other two. And this triple loss of strictness always indicates decadence.

Judged by this criterion, all India is decadent, although each region is so in its peculiar way. To take Bengal alone, of which I have complete knowledge, authentic 'Bengali-ness' in all three has not only declined, but virtually disappeared. Bengali colloquial speech, Bengali cuisine, and the Bengali costume of dhoti and a *Punjabi*, were the foundation of Bengali conservatism and identity. All three are in a state of *désarroi*, if not actually in a shambles.

Young Bengalis who visit me at Oxford remark after hearing me that I speak like their grandmothers, not even their mothers. Next, even in England, I am in my dhoti when at home, whereas even in Calcutta very few Bengalis now appear in public except in trousers or pyjamas. I am also most 'uncontemporary' in this that I sleep in a dhoti. But the contemporary Bengali libertarians in matters of clothes are nondescript. Their sartorial choice is wholly capricious. This is more or less true of Hindu life in every great city of India. The upper garment is now not even a shirt, but a T-shirt, with an inscription.

Coming finally to habits of eating, I would say that, as an indication of decadence, the changes in them in Bengal are the most significant. The Bengalis were extremely conservative both as to what they ate and how they ate it. A day on which they did not eat boiled rice, but a richer meal of *luchis* (thin and delicate roundels of white flour dough shaped by a rolling-pin, with vegetable dishes, sweet yogurt plus sweets) was called by them a day of fast. The same Bengalis nowadays relish south Indian *bhondas* and *idlis*; they have also begun to eat Chinese food as a luxury. But they have an extreme dislike for English cooking, and even French and Italian dishes. Their one-sided abandonment of conservatism in respect of eating I see as a manifestation of decadence.

A Special Bengali Feature of Decadence

Being a Bengali, I naturally feel its emergence keenly, but I am not bringing it in for that reason. It has a bearing on the pan-Indian decadence. I shall explain how.

The feature is the disintegration of the very old and stable Bengali social order which goes under the name of '*bhadralok*'. Its exact equivalent both semantically and socially is the English word 'gentlefolk'. The word is in Shakespeare (see *Richard III*, Act I, Sc.1, l. 95).

The origin of the Bengali 'bhadralok' class goes back to the twelfth century. It soon became the highest class in Bengali society. In the nineteenth century its sense of solidarity was reinforced by pride, for it was this class which created the culture now recognized as the modern Indian culture. Thus, the passing away of the Bengali bhadralok order is the extinction of the creators of that culture. Sadly, even the culture is keeping the company of its creators.

The Bengali bhadralok class was in every way like the English gentry. Both regarded the general mass of their people as the 'lower classes', and considered themselves as the real, if not the only, Englishmen/Bengalis.

There were, of course, immense differences of wealth and social position among both, but the special characteristics of the Bengali bhadralok order was that within it money did not create any social division. Rich or poor, the bhadralok was a bhadralok, by birth. The status that birth gave him could not be taken away from him.

Thus, even the wealthiest bhadralok would not object to taking a bride for his son from a poor bhadralok family, provided the family had 'blood', and the girl beauty. To give only one example, Rabindranath Tagore, the son of a great landowner with an income of nearly half-a-million rupees, was married to the daughter of the bailiff of his father's estate. And just as the family found no difference in her manners, she also took her place in the family of her father-in-law without self-consciousness. She never developed any inferiority complex.

The only thing which could deprive a bhadralok of his status was going into trade. Then he had to call the landowning bhadralok 'Babu'—Master, as did the lower classes.

This massive solidarity of the class, which wholly ignored money, has now disappeared. The process began in the twenties of this century, when I noticed it with indignation. But its completion was brought about in three stages by political events. The first of these was the inauguration of provincial self-government introduced in 1937, which was granted by the Government of India Act of 1935. This created opportunities for acquiring wealth for Bengalis which never existed before. The second opportunity for becoming wealthy, and on a spectacular scale, was created by the War, which needed suppliers and offered contracts. The process was completed by the achievement of independence in 1947. All ambitious Indians, including Bengalis, regarded political power as a means of getting rich quickly.

This has created a class of new rich Bengalis whose snobbery has split the old bhadralok into two classes, not only disparate, but hostile to each other. Those who have remained poor are now a rancorous rabble. And one might say that their rancour is more or less justified by the manner of the Bengali *nouveaux-riches*.

I shall give a few examples, all authentic. A lady of this class has come to visit a family which still retains the old bhadralok character. She is seen at the end of her visit to go to a window and look down on the street below. When asked by a boy of the host's family what she was looking for, she replied: 'My Mercedes-Benz.' Bengalis of this class who come to England by air tell me that they have travelled 'Business Class'. All of them mention the names of the great hotels in which they have been put up; of course, these are all five-star.

On their part, the Bengalis who are poor by *status*, even though not for want of money, nurse unappeasable class hatred and dream of revolution. I once asked one of these revolutionaries what he was doing to bring it about. He replied: 'My wife says that I snarl in my sleep.' It is to this level that the disintegration of the old bhadralok class has sunk. I call it decadence.

As a cultural satellite of the War, India was bound to share its decadence. But there is a difference between the two manifestations. The Western rouses a civilized man to anger; the Indian benumbs him into despair.

Chapter 4

Decadence in the United States

I do not think I have to give a detailed description of the American decadence as I have of the English. The English is a derivative of the American, and the original, generally, is sharper that the copy. But I do not have the same first-hand knowledge of American decadence as I have of the English, although I have visited the United States three times, and once stayed at Austin in Texas for six months as a visiting professor.

Withal, I have a notion that the American decadence does not exhibit some of the most malignant features of the English, for example rape with murder of the victims. For this I have an explanation. Among the American people the bond of marriage has become so loose that there is no need to go to the most brutal extreme of lust in order to satisfy it.

I have very recently read a newspaper report which made me realize with what apprehension of its transience the Americans now regard the married state. A firm of jewellers has discovered that young people who are going to marry are unwilling to spend the large sum of money which is needed to buy a 22-carat engagement and wedding ring, so, they have offered to supply the ring on a weekly rent.

During our visits to the United States my wife and I were surprised to learn from many young women that they were separated from their husbands, and were now only 'friends'. Even young children said that their mother was separated from their father.

We had to hear this even in England. Once my wife and I were dining at the Ritz with a very distinguished Englishman. A young American girl was also a guest. Suddenly, she pointed at a table and said, 'Oh, there is my second husband; that is, who was!'

But it is precisely this disarray of marriage which is the greatest revolution in the mores of the American people, which I regard as a feature of their decadence. I do not understand this, however. Why and how did it come about? Marriage was the most stable human relationship among the American people. Even down to the third quarter of the nineteenth century, marriage was assumed to be so indissoluble that a young wife who discovered that her husband was intolerable in every way would still live with him, and not seek a divorce.

Traditional Marriage Among Americans: Described in a Great Novel Published in 1881

It is *The Portrait of a Lady* by Henry James. I regard it as one of the greatest novels in the English language, also as a true account of the traditional American marriage. If anybody could be relied upon to give a true account of it, it was Henry James. He himself said in the preface he wrote for the revised 1908 edition of the novel that the question was: 'Is it valid, in a word is it genuine, is it sincere, the result of some direct impression or perception of life?'

I have no hesitation in saying emphatically that this novel was. I ask every young woman of today who considers herself intelligent and independent in spirit to read the book in order to ponder over the question whether she would not be taken in by an unscrupulous adventurer.

In this novel, Isabel Archer, who is depicted as the highest example of this type of young American woman, is led into marriage by two highly sophisticated American expatriates—one a woman and the other a man, without being aware on account of her confidence in her own intelligence that she was being exploited. The man whom she marries is as calculating as he is refined. It is not that he is incapable of love, but that he is equally incapable of forgetting self-interest. He can keep love under the strict control of calculation. He succeeds and lives with Isabel in a palace in Rome. It should be mentioned that Isabel was immensely wealthy through a legacy from her uncle, as she thought. This was the essential consideration with her suitor.

It did not take a long time for Isabel to realize that she had made a mistake. Her marriage had reached such a stage within a few years that when one day she entered her husband's study on a very urgent business without knocking at the door, he said: 'When I come to your room I always knock.'

She explained that she had forgotten because she was very upset after receiving a message from England that her cousin was dying. She added that she wished to go to England to see him.

Her husband curtly forbade it. He was very calm in his manner, but stern in his intention. After some argument conducted in the same style between the two, Isabel said: 'I suppose that if I go you'll not expect me to come back.' He replied: 'Are you out of your mind?'

She of course went, after having told him when he accused her of being calculating: 'It's your own opposition that's calculated. It is malignant.' His last words were: 'I really can't argue with you on the hypothesis of your defying me.'

Nevertheless, she acted according to her decision. After the death of her cousin, one of her friends advised her not to go back but also tried to reassure her by saying that her husband might not make a scene. She replied very calmly: 'He will, though it won't be the scene of a moment; it will be a scene of the rest of my life.'

Yet, she went back, but why?

If anyone wants to understand why Henry James made her go, he should read what Alexis de Tocqueville wrote about the attitude of young women in America to marriage in the second volume of his famous work, *Democracy in America*, published in 1842. It is to be found in Chapter 10 of Part 3 of the work, and is entitled: 'Comment la jeune fille retrouve sons les traits de l'épouse' ('How does a young woman find her bearings in her character as wife').

I give my translation of the passage:

> Since in America paternal discipline is very lenient and the married relationship very strict, a young woman contracts marriage with circumspection as well as fear. In American society one sees very few precocious marriages. American women do not marry until their reason is trained and mature; whereas elsewhere the great majority of women begin to exercise their reason and make it mature only after marriage.

Tocqueville emphasizes that this is not imposed on the young women. They impose it on themselves, with the sole effort of their own will. Then he sets down:

> When the time comes to choose a husband, this cool and austere reasoning which a liberal view of life has made clear and firm, teaches young American women that a light and independent spirit within the marriage bond is the source of eternal trouble, not of pleasure; that the amusements of a young girl cannot continue as the dalliances of a wife; and that for a woman the source of happiness is in the conjugal abode. Seeing in advance and clearly which is the way that leads to family happiness, she enters it with her first step, without seeking to return to her former ways.

This view of the man–woman relationship is also expounded in a very subtle way by Henry James in another novel of his, *The Europeans*. It is a very sophisticated and beautiful story, and I cannot explain why it has been virtually neglected by literary critics.

The dramatic time of the story is the fifties of the nineteenth century and the dramatic personae are a typical New England family and two expatriate Americans, who have so thoroughly Europeanized themselves that they intersperse their conversation very liberally with French words and phrases. To heighten the contrast further the elder expatriate, a sister, is married morganatically to a German prince and holds the rank of Baroness. The younger brother is a painter, and calls himself a Bohemian. He is always blithe, and is in addition very handsome.

The family has its imposing, spacious, and very lighted home in a typical New England village, seven-and-a-half miles westward of Boston. I went to such a village in 1972 and at once became conscious of the New England scene and spirit. So was Tagore, when he went to such a village near Boston in 1913. Since he had felt the same as I did, New England life seems to have remained intact till today.

After the sister and brother had paid their first visit to their New England relatives, the head of the family, Mr Westworth admonished his family:

> You must be careful, You must keep watch. This is a great change, and we are to be exposed to peculiar influences. I don't say they are bad; I don't judge them in advance. But they may perhaps make it necessary that we should exercise wisdom and self-control. It will be a different tone.

The old man's cautious anticipation was fully justified by the event. His brilliant second daughter and the brilliant painter cousin fell in love with each other. It was a very delicate situation. But the two looked at it differently, the Europeanized painter like a European and the girl as an American.

Once, when the young man was in the garden late at night, the girl came out to talk to him. The young man said: 'I have a little of a bad conscience. I oughtn't to meet you in this way till I have got your father's consent.' The girl replied: 'I don't understand you. We have done nothing but meet since you came here—but meet alone. What is the difference now? Is it because it is at night?' The young man replied: 'The difference is that I love you more, more than before.'

I am quoting all this to put to others the most insistent question that is in my mind. What has happened since the late nineteenth century in the United States that this old-established mode of thinking about the man–woman relationship has gone overboard; it is the converse of throwing the tea-chests into the sea in Boston. It is a total abandonment of the American *Mos majorum*—the way of the ancestors.

I shall not write more about decadence in America. What has happened to the institution of marriage is enough to establish the case for American decadence.

I shall next consider the most important question that this decadence raises—what effect can the extraordinary capacity of the American people in technology have on the progress of the human decadence?

Meaning of the Word Technology

I have just said that I have to consider next the connection between the decadence in America and American technology, as well as the indisputable superiority of Americans in this.

The statement lacked the precision which I have laid down for myself as the first desideratum for this book, so that there might not be any justification for a reader to misunderstand me unintentionally. So, I must first of all find the exact meaning of the word as given in the dictionaries I am using. And to being with, I have to give its history.

In its first half—techno—which is the substantive component, it is derived from the Greek word *techne*, which means a craft. Thus a carpenter is called a *tekton*.

The word in Greek is an exact equivalent of the Sanskrit root *taks* (तक्ष) and the Sanskrit noun *taksah* (तक्ष:), which respectively mean to carve and carpenter.

In its modern form, the compound 'technology' has shed its lowly denotation. It is a neologism; its first citation in the *OED* dates from 1625, when it meant a discourse or treatise on the practical or industrial arts. Its general extension to all practical and industrial arts collectively dates from 1839.

In current usage it means the practical application of scientific knowledge in order to make things or obtain practical results from it. Primarily, it is applied to handling matter, but very recently it has had a biological extension.

Why Americans are its Supreme Practitioner

The first reason is that they are drawn to it by their national prepossessions. Alexis de Tocqueville, with his natural perspicacity saw it, and described it as follows:

The intellect can, it seems to me, divide science in three parts. The first part contains the most theoretical principles, the most abstract notions, whose application is not known at all, or is far distant.

The second part contains the general truths which in spite of their derivation from pure theory, nevertheless leads to practice by a direct and short route.

The third part consists in finding the processes and means of execution.

He continued:

In America the purely practical part of science is admirably cultivated, and there is attention to the theoretical portion of science only to the extent required for application.

This attitude, Tocqueville said, is in total contrast to the aristocratic attitude, which gives a natural impulse to the mind to seek the highest levels of thought and disposes it naturally to develop a sublime and almost divine love of truth. The scientists of an aristocratic society, Tocqueville further added, have a thoughtless contempt for the practical application of science.

Tocqueville found this contempt in the ancient Greek scientist, mathematician and Doric aristocrat, Archimedes.

In popular legends in ancient times, he was credited with inventing some destructive engines of war; he did. But he never left any written documents. All his works are abstract scientific treatises.

On Archimedes, Tocqueville cited Plutarch, who wrote:

Archimedes was so high-minded that he never condescended to leave in writing any work on how to make those machines of war; he regarded all practical inventions as vile and mercenary, and he dedicated his mind only to those things whose beauty and subtlety were in no way mingled with any necessity.

Tocqueville found an additional reason for the American preference of the practical side of science in their taste for material welfare. He wrote that he had not met an American, however poor he might be, who did not cast a hopeful and envious glance at the enjoyments of the rich, and whose imagination did not seize in advance the good things of life which fate obstinately refused him. Tocqueville's final observation on this American aspiration was as follows:

> Love of the material enjoyments of life has become a national and dominant inclination: the strong current of a human passion leads them in that direction; it drags them in its course.

American Technology and Civilized Standard of Living

The love of 'material enjoyments' of which Tocqueville wrote, set the Americans on a course of invention which created what is now regarded as modern civilized life. It cannot be lived in its externals without a very large number of scientific appliances. Let me first enumerate those that make home life easy and comfortable, and not only make it far less laborious than before, but also bring a number of amenities in it. A housewife is now very houseproud and takes as great a pride in her kitchen as in her drawing room:

1. The very first of the new conveniences, which is also a great amenity, is electric lighting, made possible by the invention of the incandescent bulb by Thomas Alva Edison in 1879.

What electric light could do for an ancient and gloomy English country house is described in a famous story by Arthur Conan Doyle, *The Hound of the Baskervilles*. Sir Henry Baskerville, the young heir who has come from Canada, is very much depressed by the avenue which leads to the house from the lodge. He says:

> It's enough to scare any man. I'll have now a row of electric lamps and you won't know it again with a thousand-candle power Swan and Edison in front of the hall-door.

But the evidence is not from fiction only; it also comes from actual living. Viscount Scarsdale introduced electricity soon after in his stately Adams house—Kedleston Hall—and his son, Lord Curzon, installed it in Government House, Calcutta, in 1899, which was built in imitation of Kedleston by Wellesley.

Electric lighting spread quickly in India. I saw it for the first time in January 1904, in Mymensingh town. It was supplied to Maharaja

Suryakanta's Swiss chalet from a private generator in the park. Later in the same year, I saw S. Roy's shop of sports goods in Calcutta lighted up by pretty clusters of electric lamps.

I shall now mention the other inventions in their order of importance, disregarding chronology:

2. The vacuum cleaner (Hoover).
3. The sewing machine (Singer).
4. The refrigerator (Frigidaire).
5. The telephone (Bell).
6. The gramophone (Edison).

For the office came (7) the typewriter (Remington). And air travel was made possible by the building of (8) the first heavier-than-air flying machine by the Brothers Wright in 1903. I first saw an aeroplane rising from the ground in the racecourse in Calcutta in 1910.

Only the motor-car driven by an internal-combustion engine was not an American invention.

Technology and Decadence

These are very impressive, and not only impressive but revolutionary, achievements of technology, which could be expected to create a new style of living. They have, but only in externals. If my hypothesis of decadence be correct, the technological aids to living have not made it immune to decadence, not only in the United States, but all over the world. Everywhere, as it seems to me, the new style of living created by technology is coexistent with decadence. This is the most baffling paradox in human life ever seen in history. Why should scientific inventions have failed to inject a new vitality into human existence? I cannot give the reason, but I can describe the paradoxical situation.

First, the most striking paradox is that of all people, the people of the United States should exhibit decadence, and that also in its most dogmatic form. Not less paradoxical is the fact that the latest decadence in history, which is universal, has its centre of diffusion in the United States.

I say this because the Americans are the youngest nation in Western history. They came into existence only in 1776, and what they created was a local version of European civilization. Yet they *are* decadent.

On this analogy the Germanic peoples, who after the decline of the Graeco-Roman civilization took it over, should have become decadent by the time Charlemagne came to represent the Roman Empire. Instead, his age saw the emergence of modern European civilization in its first recognizable form. Therefore it was called the Carolingian renaissance.

Nothing explains this paradox in America, but paradox it is. I became conscious of decadence in America when I went there for the first time in 1971, and during a lengthy visit in 1972. I saw it in its Hispano-American form at Austin (Texas) and in its Anglo-American form in Boston and Philadelphia. Both the latter cities struck me as being 'run-down' places.

In Boston, I felt that I was seeing the throwing down of tea-chests into the Bay in its reverse. Then something from England was being jettisoned; in 1972 it seemed to me that something in America was being thrown down. It was the Anglo-American civilization in its established form.

But decadence today is not exclusively American, nor is it like the manifestations of decadence previously known. It is an absolutely new form of decadence, and its newness lies in the fact that it is being seen in an age when the whole economic basis of civilization has changed, and also become more favourable to it.

Till the middle of the eighteenth century, the economic basis of all civilization in the world was agriculture, accompanied by handicrafts. All the previous decadences occurred within that economic period. The present one is occurring in the age of machines. With their help, production of consumer goods has multiplied astronomically both in quality and variety. This economic revolution is complete in the West, and is being fostered both in Asia and in Africa by the Western countries. Yet the countries and peoples of both the continents, some highly civilized from very ancient times, some primitive, have caught the contagion of the Western decadence. The absolutely new power of making things established in the West and spreading rapidly and irresistibly all over the world is not making any difference to the expansion of Western decadence everywhere. What is called Hindu and Islamic fundamentalism is the resistance of the old Hindu and Islamic cultures both to modernization of human life and to Western decadence. But these are retrogressive movements with no prospects in the future except a fossilified continuation. So, decadence may now be said to be triumphant, no longer militant.

But there is still another extension of technology to consider. It is the discovery and application of nuclear power. This is usually regarded as an American achievement. But really it is American only in its practical extension, not in the discovery of its fundamental theoretical principles. That was European.

The United States was entrusted with the practical extension of the theory of nuclear energy for reasons connected with World War II. Up to its outbreak, both Britain and Germany found the immediate necessities of war production so over-burdening that the governments of these countries could not afford either the money or the manpower needed to utilize nuclear power for the War. Hitler stopped all research and work on this in Germany, Britain deliberately transferred the burden to the United States. That was why the Americans were first in the field to employ atomic power to conduct and end the War.

The Soviet Union followed and succeeded in 1951; probably, China also has; Israel almost certainly has, perhaps also India. Other countries are trying.

The practical application of nuclear power had two objects: first, manufacture of the most destructive weapon for waging war; secondly, space research. In both, the United States is far ahead of the other parties. It is a competition for power.

But in this there is a difference between the United States and the others. The latter have almost the sole aim of acquiring a weapon of war, and the other aims as pretexts. The United States has the weapon but is now concentrating on space research. In this field it has achieved spectacular success; it has landed man on the moon and sent rockets past the solar system.

The results achieved in this effort are different. In the military application the weapon was made so destructive that its employment in war became inconceivable to the two great powers—the United States and the erstwhile Soviet Union. Thus the nuclear bomb became a deterrent of war. As such, it has ensured peace between the great powers for over fifty years, a state of international relations never before seen in history over nearly five thousand years. For this humanity should be grateful to the nuclear bomb, instead of staging foolish demonstrations against it.

Through space research, on the other hand, nuclear power is giving man a knowledge of the universe unobtainable till now. How much more will be gained is impossible to say at present.

Both these results have to be seriously considered in dealing with the phenomenon of decadence. I hold very unorthodox views on the subject. I think the military employment of the nuclear weapon has become impossible. If any of the minor countries employ it out of sheer vindictiveness, they would be punished; but I think even these countries wish to have the weapon as a deterrent and not for employment.

As regards space research, its results can be nothing but beneficial for mankind, enabling man to orient himself in the Cosmos correctly.

Yet, nuclear achievement is not making any impact on the progress of decadence. The reason is more or less easy to discover, provided one has the wish to look for it. It is to be found in the fact that nuclear power belongs to the latest industrial basis of human existence, whereas civilization belongs to the old agricultural basis. Therefore, civilization is still repeating its old life-cycle unaffected by the new technology.

There is nothing to prevent the independent operation of the two. This has created an unprecedented psychological situation for man. To a man who has an objective historical outlook the future of human existence has become very uncertain, and unpredictable at this moment of history. On the other hand, among Americans and, following their example, among some Europeans, including the English, decadence has come to be regarded as the normal condition of human life, though not the most desirable. There is fanaticism behind decadence, a form of hubris never seen before. This makes decadence capable of subjugating the human mind. It can be personified as the contemporary form of the Greek goddess Circe.

Homer related that she lived on her island, sweetly singing before her loom, taking in those who came to her door; she gave them seats, served them food, in which she mixed the drug that turned them into brute beasts. The Americans now are at her door, and an American Polites is crying, out: 'Friends, there is somebody within singing sweetly. Come quickly and cry aloud to her.'

But I see it differently, and I believe it is real. So the leitmotif of this book is the note of despair: 'There are tears of things, and they touch the heart of mortal man.'

Everything beyond is uncertain, and the foreground is *vide et méant*, empty with nothingness in it. I wish I could see man's great age coming anew—it may; but I cannot see how it will.